MEMOIRS OF MR AVERAGE

by

M.E.LEWIS

CHAPTER 1 – THE GREEN GODDESS

I was born on 19th January 1963, one of the harshest winters since 1740. Raised at number 260 New Cheltenham Road, Kingswood, a suburb of Bristol.

Being born in that winter must be the reason I dislike the cold so much, or it could have been the shivering winters in that old house in New Cheltenham Road. With no central heating and the old metal casement windows that rattled in the wind, the ice would form on the inside as well as the outside of the windows and you could see your breath in the cold when you rose from your sleep on the winter mornings. Extra warmth came in the form of a crochet blanket, knitted by one of my sisters, made up from left over pieces of wool from jumpers and scarves knitted by my mother.

It was always hard to get out of bed on those frosty mornings and, like most, I don't like the cold. I would rather go to Hell than go skiing; it would be a lot warmer!

I was the youngest of seven children, but the first to be born in a hospital. My eldest sister Ann, the first born to my mother Iris Lewis, came into the world delivered not by a midwife, but by my mother herself! My father Ernie had gone to fetch the midwife, but by the time he arrived home my sister had already been born!

My mother was a kind and generous woman, yet made of all the right stuff! She was no stranger to hardship, having been weathered by two world wars.

She and her Brother Ted grew up on a small farm holding in Kingswood, Bristol. Life was simple, making money from vegetables and chickens, after her father returned from Russia in the First World War.

Tormented by his trials in Russia, the rural life would be the path he desired. He could now eat fresh eggs and fresh vegetables instead of his often diet in the trenches of horse, or anything thing else available for that matter.

Needless to say, my mother's father was the strict type, as in the army discipline would have been paramount in the running of his house and business. He trusted nobody, and kept his money in a bag that was tied to a piece string, which he would then toss in a hole in the floor boards away from prying eyes!

Married to my Nan Olive, with his trustworthy sheepdog Bruce by his side, Edward was a big framed man, six foot six with hands like shovels and dressed in a collarless shirt and bracers, the sort of man who would polish his boots daily in front of the fire. He was sometimes over protective of his daughter and would send Bruce the dog to wait for her at the end of the street, should she venture out with friends. He refused to let her join the Land Army in the Second World War - his word was final!

I still have a lighter he made from two pennies, in the trenches in Russia, which my mother handed to me a long time ago. I think lighters must have been preferred to light cigarettes rather than matches in the trenches.

There's a saying that a third light from a match is unlucky! This stems back from the trenches of the First World War. It is said that when you struck the match the enemy would see it and take up his gun. When you passed it on to the second soldier, the enemy would take aim, and when the second soldier passed it on to the third soldier, the enemy would fire!

It's funny how fate and destiny can affect future generations; the unpredictable toils of war and the effect it has on humanity.

It strikes me funny that most war memorial statues commemorating the war, are those of men wielding guns, but the harsh reality is that so many were only teenagers; the average age of the soldier being from sixteen to twenty four.

A telegram to my mother nearing the end of the Second World War could have changed everything for her forever. She had met a marine in the war's infant days; a tall dark haired man whose name was Sid and she fell hopelessly in love with him, but then the day came when he was drafted back to war. It was a common affair for the young men of England to leave their families and lovers to go to war and fight for king and country, in fact they didn't have much choice in the matter.

Iris and Sid kept in touch writing letters to each other, but his replies became scarcer as the war intensified with Germany, until the replies from him eventually stopped.

She kept writing to him, hoping for one day a response, but nothing came from the postman. Day after day she would wait sitting at the bottom of the stairs for a delivery of mail, but still nothing came.

Fearing the worst she had to come to terms that he was lost in action and, with time being the greatest of healers, she put it behind her and began to reconstruct her life over.

It was in this period that she met my father Ernie. It was common place to get married quickly in the war, as the men were never home for long periods of time and you would have to live every day as if it was your last, because of course, it could have been.

So on 8th April 1943 my mother and father married and resided to live with his parents in Alsop Road, Kingwood. Her marine lover Sid had now been forgotten.

Then one summer's morning the postman arrived with a telegram while she was at her mother's house. At first she thought it was bad news concerning her brother Ted who was at war in Europe, but as she began to read on she realised it was a telegram from the marine she thought dead.

It read;

"Dear Iris, I am sorry it has taken so long to write to you. I have been in a prisoner of war camp, and myself and some of the other men have escaped.
I am back in England and I would so much like to meet up with you. I will be in the Inn by Temple Meads Train Station at midday, please come and meet me."

A wave of emotions came upon her; she was speechless to say the least.

My father Ernie had known of the marine and made her burn any letters or photos she had from him in the past, but he never knew about what happened later that day.

Not knowing what to do, she confided in her mother Olive. *"We must go and meet him. We can't just ignore it."* explained Olive.

So they both headed off into town to meet the man she thought was dead. I can imagine how she looked, her dark hair in the bang style of the time, her legs stained with tea to make them look tanned, and a mascara line painted up the back of her legs to give the impression of stockings; common practice by women of the 40's.

As they walked into the bar he was sat upright in the corner with his uniform on, without a hair out of place. A little thinner now, but still the same half smile he always had before he was shipped to war. His face lit up with excitement as she walked towards him and he stood up to greet them and set about ordering some drinks for them. Feeling rather nervous she didn't know what drink to have, so he told her, *"Leave it with me Iris, I will get you a drink fit for a queen."*

On his return from the bar he handed Olive a stout and my mother a cocktail called the Green Goddess; a mixture of banana, melon, liqueur, and milk and green in color.

After an awkward thirty minutes and hearing of his escape from the prisoner of war camp, she began to tell him, with tears rolling down her face, clutching her handkerchief close to her mouth, as she always did when she was upset, that she still felt the same, but fearing he was killed in action she had moved on and married someone else.

"But why didn't you wait for me?" he asked. She was overcome with remorse and guilt and being too upset to even talk, Olive explained how she had written many letters and had eventually given up hope.

He stood up, clearly upset, but with dignity he explained, *"Enjoy the Green Goddess Iris, and I will marry the first lady I meet on the train home,"* and he left.

Some time later my mother found out from a friend that on his train journey home he had indeed met a lady, a nurse, and he married her.

Maybe it was the thought of my mother Iris that kept him going in the prisoner of war camp? I can only imagine what the marine had felt on that day, but maybe he had my mother to thank for his escape?

I decided to write this book for many reasons; I've tried to be honest and true in my writings. I am just an average man, from an average town, and an average family and upbringing.

I wanted this book to be a voyeuristic look into family and friends' lives and times; a social history.

All the people I mention in this book I've been lucky to have been enriched by them. All the people that I haven't mentioned, maybe I will write more memoirs in the future; god knows I could write volume after volume about the people I've been lucky enough to be around.

I mention lots of music references in this book; it's music that has really inspired me throughout my life. I find music not only the universal language, but it's like a trigger in your head, when you hear a piece of music it triggers thoughts from the past, whether good or bad, happy or sad. It has real meaning in all its shapes and forms.

Ernie Lewis

Iris Lewis

CHAPTER 2 - BEST DAYS OF YOUR LIFE?

In the 70's and 80's everybody seemed to work in a factory. It was the backbone of the industrial world we had created here in England.

I started my working days at a builders' merchant's warehouse stacking toilets and moving heavy cast concrete fireplaces around. It was a hard and physical job and my foreman was a man I called Paddington. He was a small thin man and aged in his sixties; he wore bib and braces overalls and was a bit too old to lift things himself, so he just told you where everything had to go.

The thing that struck me funny with Paddington was that he had a boy racer car; it was an old Cortina and had leopard skin seats, furry dice in the window, and go faster stripes on the body work. It was the kind of car that you would expect an eighteen year old to drive. It was most odd!

It was on a bus journey to the yard on 2nd February 1979 that I learnt of the death of John Simon Richie, better known for his stage name of Sid Vicious, bass player with The Sex Pistols. He had died from an overdose of drugs whilst on bail for the murder of his girlfriend Nancy Spungen. I couldn't believe it; it made the front page of every tabloid. It was one of those pieces of news that you remember where you were and what you were doing at the time; it was the death of a punk rock hero of mine at the time.

After leaving the warehouse job to work in Bendix Weston House in Kingswood, I couldn't believe the difference in wages.

I had been paid seventeen pounds a week at the warehouse and, after paying my house keep of a fiver, it didn't leave me much money to squander. At the factory my wages jumped to seventy pounds per week.

I remember feeling a bit of a dunce working in an engineering factory, at Bendix Weston House. I was making airbrakes on the production line. Formerly the factory was called Douglasses, where they made motorbikes and airplane wings in the Second World War. It kind of made you feel a bit worthless working in a factory, it had stigma to it, clocking in and out each ground hog day. I can still remember my clocking in number to this day, three five zero seven. I had become a number for the first time; but not the last!

But the money was good and I upped my housekeep and could afford to splash out on some new bondage trousers and mohair jumpers from a shop in the centre of Bristol called Paradise Garage. It was a great shop that sold all alternative clothes; great winkle picker shoes, leather jackets, and just about everything a punk rocker could ask for. With the music from Public Image playing in the back ground, it was one cool shop to be seen in.

Factories were breeding grounds for petty arguments between the workers, and also a militant stomping ground. It was repetitive work and extremely boring for most. The smell of coolant, a liquid that was used on the engineering lathes to keep them cool, would linger on your clothes. If you bumped into an old friend on your way home, he didn't have to ask where you worked; he could smell it!

Every now and again the management would come up with some sort of rule or regulation that would upset everyone. I could never understand why the management would keep introducing petty rules for things.

The great leader Abraham Lincoln once said, "*A house divided by itself cannot stand.*" or in my words, "A Good work force is a happy one."

At nine thirty every morning the tea trolley came along and a queue was quickly formed, waiting to get something to eat. The food was subsidised by the factory so it was cheap to buy.

Women had not long been granted equal pay, and the semi-skilled scheme also had not long been introduced, which caused a few debates on the factory floor from time to time. The older men thought of this as not right for women to have equal pay for some reason, they thought that a woman earning as much as them was in some way derogative to men.

As for myself I thought it only fair and for the first time my own mother was not chained to the kitchen sink at home, she was back out to work cleaning and never happier.

The women who worked at Bendix Engineering were the strong type and wouldn't take any messing from the moaning and groaning of the senior men. In fact if you ask me the older men were scared of these feisty working women, and to be honest in Union disputes they had more back bone than the men.

This was of course thanks to the women of Dagenham Ford Motor Company in Essex who went on strike in June 1968.

As much as I hated factory life back then, I would give anything now to see factories re-open their gates again. They were safe houses. Things like a steady income in the form of a brown paper wage packet, handed to you by the foreman on pay day, a pension and your fees to the Union to keep the bosses in check, are now a thing of the past in most jobs. There were no signs of greedy bankers in sight and the majority of people rented accommodation from the once mighty council.

When eventually your wages had to be paid into the bank with no choice in the matter, that's when things took a turn for the worse in my opinion. Before long most fell foul, including me, to the overdraft facility and bank charges. We began to live beyond our means and the introduction of privatisation by the late Margret Thatcher has had its pitfalls right up to the present day.

The coal mining towns were worst hit, leaving whole towns unable to find work.

My father Ernie would tell me, *"Son, a pound of your own is worth two of anyone else's."* if only I would have listened to him!

An interesting man I worked with at the factory was a gentleman by the name of Morley Bailey. He had grey swept back hair, a barrel chest and a scar that started from the top of his left eyebrow and carried on right down the side of his face. He looked like a gangster from one of the old 50's movies. Strong as an ox, he could lift a seventeen foot scaffold pole into the air from one end. I don't know how he got the scar but you didn't ask Morley too many questions, as he was scary at times.

Morley escaped death in the Second World War when a bomb had a direct hit on his neighbour's house.

One look from him would turn your blood cold if he disapproved of something, but for some strange reason he took to me. We became good friends and he became my mentor.

I used to drink with him at The Gin Palace in Old Market, the old centre of Bristol, from time to time. It was an odd public house; the décor reminded me of a fairground ride, with ornate wood carvings painted in gold everywhere and large red velvet curtains. In the 60's they filmed a Carry On film there. The floor sloped away from you in the bar as you walked in, and it was full of characters.

Morley would stand at the end of the bar, as if in command of the whole pub, with his barrel chest out whilst the barman stood cleaning the glasses with a tea towel. There was a lady in her late fifties who sat on a high stool. She had jet black hair in the style of Audrey Hepburn, lots of red rouge and red lipstick and a tight black pencil skirt and stockings. She constantly had a cigarette in her mouth, rolling it from the left corner to the right corner of her mouth and back again with her tongue; she was memorizing. The ashtray was never far from her, and the cigarette ends she had extinguished were caked with lipstick.

Morley always looked after me and never let me spend any money; he always carried a big roll of cash with him. I don't know why he worked at the factory; he was certainly not short of money.

Shady characters would come in the bar with their collars up carrying packages and hand them to the barman and leave. I thought it best not to ask any questions as nobody took any notice at all and, to be honest, I was too scared to ask.

Morley once showed me some pictures of when he fought in Korea in the 50's; they were shocking to say the least, not nice at all! The pictures were taken when they had caught some of the enemy steeling food from their camp while they were on exercises in the jungle. I cannot even bring myself to explain what they were like, or why Morley wanted to keep them – and as I said no-one messed with Morley!

In work we would sit around an old tea chest playing cards at break times to pass the time. Morley's teacup was black on the inside, he would never wash it out and if you washed it out for him you would be in big trouble. It was the way he liked it, he said it gave flavor. He would bring bread, cheese, and a raw onion wrapped in brown paper and proceed to cut off chunks of cheese and onion with his pen knife, as we played cards for a few pennies.

He would never attend any Union meetings on the shop floor and kept himself to himself. If you needed money, you asked Morley. If you had trouble with the foreman, you would go to Morley. Do you get the picture?

Now it can't go unmentioned, there was a man called Ron at the factory who was older and had a hunch on his back. He was in charge of maintaining the machines. He wore a dark blue boiler suit, had white brylcreem slapped back hair, teeth like a piano, and was always polishing his spanners.

Ron got his hunch on his back from stepping on a land mine in the Second World War. I loved talking to him about the war; I have always had a fascination about it ever since I wrote a poem for a school book about Poppy Day and hearing the old stories from my parents around the tea table.

I was at the grand old age of 10 when I wrote this. I was given the poem after the death of my mother Iris; she had kept it all those years.

It reads:

"Muddy ditches in the ground hold the soldiers long since dead.
There's not a sound.
The screaming shells and blundering bombs are scared to whimper anymore.
Perhaps they too are dead.
The mothers cry and grieve so much; their sons have died with the bullets touch
And now we think back to the days of death and destruction.
We remember them now on Poppy Day....."

I used to ask Ron, *"What's it like to kill someone?"* He would just smile and ask, *"What do you want to know that for?"*

When he did eventually open up, the expression on his smiling face would change; I could see it was painful for him to talk about, but I was persistent in my enquiries. He told me of a time when he was in Italy, him and his unit came across an abandoned farm house. On entering it they discovered that it had signs of occupancy, so they set up a gun in the roof space and waited for any signs of German soldiers. Later in the day Ron was manning the gun and walking up the road were several German soldiers, talking and laughing. He turned to his superior and asked, *"What shall I do?"*

"Mow em down!" was his answer. So he opened fire and killed all of them.

I asked Ron, *"What was it like?"*

He replied to me in a soft whispering voice, *"They just rolled over son, they just rolled over."*

It was a stagnant way to describe to me what happened on that day. *"They just rolled over."* I've never forgotten him saying that to me, he seemed remorseful, but it was a kill or be killed war.

I thought at the time, that is what it must be like when you are getting old, when the fire in your belly is finally extinguished, after fighting for so long, the life sucked from you like a vacuum cleaner, eventually you just give up, you roll over, and you become like an elephant tied to a stake. Stories like that tend to stick with you forever.

When I asked him about the H bomb dropped by the Americans from the airplane Enola Gay on Hiroshima, he replied, *"I was glad, they would have killed us all....."*

Ron wasn't the only war veteran I would talk to in the factory. There was a man called Clifford Fudge who was a tail gunner in a Lancaster bomber of which is in a museum in London to this day.

I cannot imagine what it must have been like sat in a tiny space at the rear of a Lancaster bomber; it must have been claustrophobic at best.

Clifford was a small and smartly dressed man with not a hair out of place, he was always smiling and nothing bothered him. I never once saw him upset or phased by anything that went on in the factory. I guess not knowing if you are going to live or die when he boarded the Lancaster on every mission must make you pretty hardened to life in general. My old work colleague, Steve Clark, visited the Lancaster in the London museum after Clifford died and found the experience very sobering.

I took to reading Karl Marks' Book of Communism in the early stages of factory life. I found the idea of communism interesting, but was not so naive to thinking it could ever work. I even went on a march through St Paul's in Bristol with a load of commies.

I think it only fair to say that, like most of us, I'm a capitalist. We all love our creature comforts, our nice cars, our holidays and our TV sets with five hundred TV channels. It seems to make us tick.

I am envious of people who don't have the constant craving for more. In fact I love to watch a good story unfold on any of the ten or more news channels.

One that sticks in my mind is the conflict in Iraq; the news went something like this;

"We are hunting down Saddam Husain's arsenal of weapons of mass destruction!"
One week later;
"We still have not found the weapons of mass destruction!"
Another week passed;
"We have found SOME weapons."

Now that news kind of left a bad taste in my mouth when it became apparent there were no weapons of mass destruction yet so many lives lost - think on.

And, what would we do without being able to record TV? I mean, who the hell wants to sit through adverts? It wouldn't be so bad if adverts were interesting. I can imagine businessmen sat in the boardroom watching an advert campaign that some guy has taken all of thirty seconds to think up and saying, *"Bravo, we will sell much more of our product now!"*

It has the opposite effect on most people - You think, *"Shit advert, shit product."* Now put a girl in a bikini, running out of the sea in slow motion, and you can sell anything!

I record any program I want to watch so I don't have to sit through these toe curling adverts; it's my time so don't waste it!

I don't think a year goes by that on the news we are told of places in Africa that have no clean water! Now I'm no rocket scientist, but if we can build a tunnel from the UK to France, send a missile through a letterbox and build a space station miles above the earth - why the hell can't we build a water pipe to Africa?

Looking on the brighter side, there's only one thing that annoys me more, and that's when I go to the barbers to get my hair cut and when the barber is finished, he grabs the mirror and shows me the back of my head, which resembles a bird's nest! Now really, who the hell wants to see the back of their head?

It's the same effect with CCTV cameras in stores, all I can see is the shiny bit on the top of my head. It's not a nice feeling walking in town these days, I feel like I'm being watched all the time, everywhere you go there are cameras. I find it intrusive and unsettling, but I guess it's a reflection of our society today.

Back at the factory; my foreman was called Ken, he walked like Charlie Chaplin, as his feet pointed at ten to two because apparently he was born with his feet the wrong way around. He had a thick head of curly brown hair and wore big spectacles like the ones you would see the Kray twins gangsters wearing in the early 60's. He was a nice bloke, but for some strange reason he would bring photos of the food he had on his holidays abroad. You see, only on foreman's wages could you afford to go abroad on holiday. Though why anyone would want to take a picture of what food they're eating baffles me?

It's a bit like why do people walk around when they are on their mobile phones? I actually saw a guy get run over while he was walking around chatting on his mobile? It also reminds me of a polar bear that used to be at Bristol Zoo, the poor bugger would just walk around and around in circles all day, it was painful to witness. At the factory I felt like taking in a photo of a cow and saying, that's what I had for tea last night.

Having said that, me and some of the other fellow workers did save up for a few days in France. There was me; Lighty, we called him that because he was big boned and a little over weight and always wore a shirt and bracers; Mousey, who was quiet and reserved; Pete Allen, who didn't need a nick name because he was the coolest guy amongst us with black hair, brown eyes and very stylish. Pete used to live three doors up from me in my infant years and even then he was cool, he was the kid who had a pair of Levis and a Ben Sherman shirt, the envy of any kid in the neighborhood; big Steve Shellard, because of course he was a strapping lad; Malcolm Towler, who was an all round good guy and loved Elvis; and Terry Rankmore who was a cool guy who always wore a waistcoat and jeans.

After months of planning and saving we set off from the port on a ferry heading for Le Havre. Now at that time public houses in the UK were strict on opening hours, so when the bar opened on the ferry after only just leaving the port, need I say we began to drink, it was like Christmas! I felt free to do what I wanted and our spirits were high.

Arriving in Le Havre at 8.00am and having no sleep at all, our first port of call was a cafe for breakfast, followed by more beer. Some of the lads jumped on the train to go sightseeing and the rest of us thought we would stay and enjoy our new found freedom.

We came across another little cafe and decided to stop there for yet more beer. It was a tiny little place, with a dark little corridor that led you into the bar area; the toilet was tiny and the toilet itself was on an angle with a chain to pull when you finished.

Sat in the corner was a woman in her fifties, caked with heavy makeup and smoking elegant super long cigarettes. She didn't take her eyes of us; it was like she was waiting for something to happen and eventually she got up from her seat and slowly walked towards us.

In broken English she asked, "*Do you boys want some business? Come with me I have lots of girls for you.*"

Now by this time we were all a bit drunk and took it as a laugh, but this lady was no pushover, she kept saying, *"Come with me, you will like very much, I have many girls for you."*

It got to a point when she was getting on everybody's nerves and Pete told her to sit down or piss off!

"Let's get the fuck out of here!" he said, and Pete being the coolest bloke on the planet, we all agreed and headed for the corridor that led us on to the street.

Now, for some strange reason, Pete grabbed a sheepskin coat off the coat hanger in the corridor and Big Steve grabbed another one and we made like John Wayne down the street laughing and falling about. I took the sheepskin coat off Big Steve and put it on, and we decided to go to the train station and catch the train elsewhere.

At the station Lighty bought a bundle of porn magazines, which was something else you couldn't get in the UK. Within minutes we were surrounded by French police armed with guns and batons; they threw us into a dark blue lock up van and out of the corner of my eye I could see the owner of the bar we had just come from being restrained by two policemen, he was screaming, *"English pigs!"* and trying his best to get at us. We sped through the streets, traffic sirens blaring.

"We are in the shit now." I said to Pete, as we arrived at the police station.

They bundled Pete, Lighty, Big Steve and me into a cell; it stank of piss and not one of the police could speak English.

After spending a few hours in the cell an officer who could speak English finally let us out to go to the captain's office to face charges of theft. On the way to his office we noticed three French policemen looking at the porn magazines Lighty had bought earlier.

"I don't think you will get them back!" I said to Lighty.

After being shouted at by the police captain in his office, we were told we would be immediately deported back to the UK and would face charges in France two weeks later.

On the journey home the sea was so rough, so I found a place on board the ferry where they kept the blankets and curled up in this little cupboard feeling sick as a dog.

Of course, none of us went back to face the music, we didn't fancy doing time in a French jail for sure.

The news spread around the factory like wild fire and on the Monday we went back to work where we had some comments like, *"I told you there would be trouble!"*, *"Bloody thugs!"* that sort of thing, but it didn't bother me or anyone else for that matter.

Back to factory life; I now realise that working in a factory was the backbone of the working class, and being working class, it's something I've always morally been proud of. If you're a foot soldier, you're a foot soldier; it rarely changes.

At present there seems to be no factories left at all, it's all shipped off to foreign countries and most phone calls you make to any British institution goes straight to India?! I've always felt that our strength as a nation was because of our position of being an island. How things have changed!

There seems to be no morals to the rich and wealthy anymore; profit is now more important than your fellow countrymen. If businessmen and women want to take their workloads to foreign countries, they should be made to live there; cheap labour and big profits are not the answer to harmony in the modern world.

At a young age at the factory I was told I had to do the night shift. This was very unpleasant, as my mates would wave me off as I left the pub at 7.30pm and carry on with their night. I felt cheated; I felt something was being taken away from me.

I could never sleep during the day. I was walking around like a zombie most of the time and the shifts were ten hours long.

I learnt quick! The operating shop I was working in was noisy when my machine was in full swing. I worked on my own for most of the night, so I devised the 'Make Like Your Working Device.'

I bought some C120 recordable cassettes which would record 120 minutes and then I recorded my machine as I worked on it. I hooked up two speakers to my cassette player and played the recording on full volume. The foreman would only come out of his office if he heard the machine stop, but my 'Make Like Your Working Device' worked like a dream. I would work half the night and play the tape the other half; this gave me a great sense of wellbeing.

When I eventually got back on working days I took it upon myself to use my old tape machine and hook it up to the tannoy speakers dotted around the shop floor and create my own radio station. I would record music at home and in between songs I would slot in adverts I had seen on TV and make the sketches amusing. For an example, I had seen a drink driving advert, so I turned it on its head and it went something like this - I acted out a man that was being pulled over by the police.

The man said, *"Officer is I pissed?"* [Slurring]

The policeman replied, *"Yes Sir, you are way over the limit!"*

The man replied, *"Thank fuck for that, I thought my steering had gone!"*

The policeman replied, *"Now blow into this............ and now into this. Thank you, I hate putting cold gloves on this time in the morning!"*

I named my radio station '*Radio C.*.N.T*'. [I have missed a vowel out for obvious reasons!]

It was the highlight of the day, that special hour at 11.00am when I would play it; it lightened the workers' mood and it was looked forward to; even the foreman found it funny. I would play classics tunes from Tom Jones and Tony Bennett to anything that sounded a bit cheesy, in between the jokes.

I had more fun with the old tape recorder. When experimenting with cannabis with my friends, I decided to secretly tape us in the car after rolling a few joints and see what it sounded like the next day.

It was a rainy night in the country lanes of Wick near Bristol that we would go to have a few smokes. So the scene was set for that night, to hide the cassette player under the car seat, unbeknown to my friends. It truly was a night I won't forget.

After smoking a few joints, I pressed the record button and sat back. Everyone was laughing and giggling as per usual, and talking complete nonsense. We set off homeward bound.

Now all of us, being high, could see things moving in the head lights and hear the occasional pop beneath the car tyres. We began to panic and stopped the car in the rain to investigate what the hell was in the road. We all got out and left the headlights on to illuminate the road.

We were faced with hundreds of frogs! All jumping around; they were everywhere. I just couldn't believe it! We all scrambled back in the car and drove off, trying to avoid all these frogs. I thought we had all lost the plot!

It wasn't until a few years later that I found out that frogs go to spawn at a certain time of year and we had witnessed this happening while high on cannabis. As for the recording, it was rather disturbing because the batteries were worn down while recording, so when I renewed the batteries the whole thing sped up and we all sounded like we had taken helium! It was very unnerving, so I destroyed it.

I spent a lot of time in Wick; it's a lovely part of the countryside. As a teenager my friends and I would cycle there and go fishing in the small river that runs through it, catching minnows and Crayfish.

It was in the country lanes of Wick that one of the funniest things happened one summer's night when I was in my late teens. Me and a friend, who's name I won't mention, had took two girls along with us in his car with intent of having some fun with them! We pulled up in a layby and there was an entrance to a corn field. We had already planned that I was to stay in the car with the girl I was with, and my mate would go into the field with the other girl.

So with the sun going down, we put our plan into action and my friend exited the car with the girl and they climbed the gate into the corn field and disappeared.

Ten minutes or so passed, and I was alerted by a farmer and his dog climbing the gate to the corn field. The farmer had not seen us in the car and we cowered behind the dashboard as not to be seen. Within minutes my friend and the girl he was with came scrambling over the gate looking all out of sorts. They jumped in the car and we sped off, and dropped the girls home. Nobody said a word all the way home. When the girls had left I asked, *"What happened in the field?"*

My friend explained to me, red faced, that he was lying with his trousers around his ankles on top of the girl when he suddenly felt a great sensation around his groin area. He was thinking to himself, *"My god this girl sure knows how to party!"*

Then he heard a cough, and to his astonishment he looked up to see a dog licking his balls and a farmer standing over them saying, *"Well, well, well, what have we got here then?"*

I've never laughed so much; it's something that still makes me smile when I think of it.

Looking back factory life wasn't so bad. Poor old Lighty passed away not long after I left; he had split with his girlfriend just before I departed, and I saw a change in him I did not like. He became miserable and short tempered. All he ever wanted was a partner, but being a bit over weight he struggled with the girls. I think she just took advantage of his kind nature and dumped him; I swear to this day he just gave up. How I see it, I think he died of a broken heart. Morley also passed away.

I do see some of the other guys from time to time. Pete moved to Germany not long after his marriage broke down and I've not seen him since.

All you ever heard in the factory was the age old saying, *"School days are the best days of your life."*
Well I for one could contest that!

Mine was not a happy one after leaving Falconride Junior School in Kingswood. I went to the Grange School for Boys in Warmley, Bristol. It was a far cry from my time spent at Falconride; which were happy days. It was all fun at junior school, and the teachers were understanding.

There was a guy in my junior class called Graham, who was of Afro Caribbean culture. He was the only black guy in the school, and as I remember it he had some anger problems. I think he lost his parents at a young age and stayed in what the teacher would call, a 'special house', so you couldn't call for him or anything like that; you just saw him in school.

I felt sorry for him a lot of the time and he didn't have any real friends. It was hard enough being the only Afro Caribbean in the whole school just for starters, and on top of that not being able to have anyone call for him to go to the park and play football or something, he must have felt very alienated and no wonder he had anger problems. He would go right off the wall at any given moment. He once punched one of the female teachers in the stomach when she was pregnant!

The male teachers handled him with force when he played up, but I used to actually look forward to him throwing a wobble, we all found it amusing. He would stomp around the playground swearing and swinging his hands around, but deep down he was in fact a nice kid and I liked him.

The teachers told him he was also going to the Grange School with us, to keep him pacified, but we never saw him again after the last day at that school and I've not seen him since.

In my last year there my teacher was a Mrs Lavis, She was as good as gold and understood the kids, and we even went to her house to carol sing in the Christmas period to earn a few pennies.

There's nothing bad to say about my junior years at all, it was all good. One thing that does stick in my mind is that one of my class mates, Lee Jarret, used to bring me in little bottles of Brut aftershave that he had stole from his older brother and I smelt like a million dollars. This aftershave was like gold dust at the time.

I only had one bit of hassle at junior school, from a kid called Mark, who was the kind of kid that although his parents were poor, would always have everything he wanted. He would manipulate other kids to be his friend by giving them sweets and inviting them around his house.

Having friends over your house was a bit of a no go to most; in general the parents could not wait to get you out of the way, so the last thing they wanted was other children in the house as well.

But this kid really got under my skin, as some of my mates could not see through him like I could and fell fowl to his antics and falling out of friends with me.

I recall one evening walking up my street and this kid was with all my mates across the road shouting names at me. I decided from that moment I would not be anybody's fool for the rest of my natural life.

I don't know what ever happened to him, but my guess is that he became a politician or something down those lines.

On my first day as a freshman at the Grange I had my first taste of what was to come.

I felt great in my new uniform my mother had bought me on hire purchase from a clothes shop in Kingswood. As I walked along the lane leading to the school I was nervous, but felt like I had all of a sudden grown up. All the older pupils looked big to me and I found this quite daunting. The school had a reputation for new pupils to be initiated by sticking their head down a toilet and pulling the flush, which was a bit worrying, but luckily this didn't happen to me.

The school was split into two; one side was boys and the other side girls. There was no interaction of boys and girls at all and if you were caught looking out of the window at the girls you would get a whack.

At break time I found myself wandering around to get some bearings of the school and couldn't wait to see the science block!

As I gingerly walked down the tarmac path leading to the science block I was approached by a smartly dressed man in a tweed jacket and brown polished leather shoes. As he walked toward me I tried to get out of his way, but he caught hold of me by the scruff of my neck and hoisted me into the air shouting, so close to my face I could smell the aroma of coffee on his breath;

"DO YOU KNOW WHO I AM BOY?" he shouted, "DO YOU KNOW WHO I AM?"

Then he threw me to the ground and marched off. I quickly learnt of Mr Lord. The rumours were he would dangle you by your feet out of the window on the top floor class room if you misbehaved and I for one believed it!

One of his infamous punishments was to make you face the blackboard and bend over while he took a run up and kicked you in the arse! All the kids were terrified of him, but I was lucky not to get him in any lessons as he taught Maths at the highest level, and that was never my strong point. Rumour had it that he was a spitfire pilot in the Second World War, but I can't be too sure.

The system was obvious even for a young lad to learn. Lessons were based on behavior. For instance, if your

Math's teacher was soft, you would get Games before your Math's lesson which was usually cross country running. This would exhaust you and therefore you would have no energy to play up in the next lesson.

In five years of that school I had one game of football!

"It's exams that count not football team's boy!" I was constantly told. Mind you I was never any good at it, but I did enjoy the game. There were privileged boys who got to play football; these were boys who had proper football boots and generally came from wealthier parents.

Having finished your Games lesson, you were then ordered to line up and run through a corridor of showers, naked! I refused to take off my shorts every time as I just didn't feel comfortable with it at all. At the other end of the showers another teacher would be waiting with a trainer to hit the kids who refused to fully undress.

It became a way of life, Games, then a beating! Looking back now, I'm older and wiser but I'm sure there was some sexual pleasure going on somewhere. And for some strange reason you were not allowed to wear underpants beneath your shorts, I also found this very odd? After running through the showers with my shorts on I would put my trousers over the top even though they were wet and I would sit in my wet shorts for the rest of the day.

There was a rumour that one of the teachers, who I won't name, hung himself while acting out a sexual affixiation in his loft. That was enough proof for me.

Another teacher was sacked for making a pupil dance around naked covered in tomato ketchup on summer camp.

Of course, being young and innocent nothing entered your mind about foul play; the word pedeophile wasn't even spoken; just maybe a warning from your parents to be on the lookout for dirty old men.

Life was tough at The Grange, not because of the kids but because of the neanderthal system and the teachers.

I once questioned the Religious Education teacher, a God fearing man, as to why dinosaurs are not mentioned in The Bible? The man made my life hell after that. Character assassination was on a daily basis, as was the rubber from a trainer shoe across your backside or a quick punch to the chest.

I saw some kids hit so hard by the trainer that they were black and blue, and couldn't sit down for days.

At the top of the punishment ladder was the cane, a thin length of bamboo about a meter long. You had to tuck your hands in when you got the cane, because if you didn't it would whip around your knuckles as you were bent over receiving the bamboo across your backside and sometimes it would whip around to your face, so you had to watch out for that as well.

Another punishment was the teacher would produce two small stones; he would make you put them on the floor, then he would make you kneel on them for the whole lesson. Barbaric!

Slaps to the head, poking you in the chest, throwing black board rubbers at you, and pulling your hair and ears, were all part of secondary education and corporal punishment.

I sometimes hear people say corporal punishment should be brought back, I just can't agree with that; I wouldn't like to see my son coming home with whale marks on his backside.

At break times the play ground and fields were patrolled by teachers on the lookout for smokers; they would even use binoculars from afar to catch a culprit.
Some kids just got on with it, but I hated every minute at the Grange School for Boys. I felt worthless there.

Outside of school was a different world. Living in Kingswood, we were surrounded by common land, a disused railway, and a quarry just down the road in Warmley. My friends and I never ventured into the town areas of Bristol; we preferred the countryside, and anyway it wasn't worth going into town unless you had money of course.

Kingswood itself formed part of the king's hunting ground in Saxon times, hence the name the King's Woods. The Saxon, King Edmond, was murdered in nearby Pucklechurch, and his son later united all the Saxon Kingdoms to become the first King of England. Edmond was Alfred the Great's grandson and frequented Pucklechurch for relaxation and hunting. The site of Edmond's Palace is said to be just outside the then forest of Kingswood in Pucklechurch, just behind The Star Inn on Castle Road.

My friends and I spent a lot of time in these areas. In the school holidays we would set off after breakfast, onwards to the vast open playground of trees, woods and fields.

We all had bird egg collections and crept about the woods and hedgerows on the lookout for birds nesting. Our code of honor was to only take one egg from each nest, so to keep the balance of nature. Only a few of us had birds of prey eggs, as they were the hardest to retrieve.

The quarry in Warmley was a place we frequented a lot. Long abandoned, it was full of water and about an acre in size; in places it was very deep. There were all sorts of junk cluttered along its banks. Oil form barrels of waste lay leaking into the water, and rusty metal of all shapes and sizes lay on the banks. It was a forbidden place to go from my parents' point of view. A friend of my brothers who lived just up the road from me drowned there. I was always warned the weeds had dragged him under. But being abundant in wildlife it was hard to stay away from there. Snakes, lizards, dragon flies, and bird life in all form could be found here. We even caught a bat in a fishing net one summer's evening as the sun was setting.

On a school trip with an art teacher to the quarry one afternoon, I made a class mate jump down a ledge to catch a grass snake I had seen going under a rusty piece of tin. He fell and broke his arm and I was punished by the usual and now familiar cane!

The teacher who took us there was an art teacher called Mr Watt; he was one of the good teachers at the school, totally eccentric, drove an old Austin Cambridge motor car and polished it at every chance he got.

He once took us to Stowe fair, where gypsies sold horses and animals over a few days. The town was taken over by gypsies, it was colorful and lawless.

At the quarry in 1980 we even used the area for planting cannabis. It was a dangerous place to go, but exciting.

The old abandoned railway lines backed on to the quarry and held many adventures for us. It was our hunting ground with our air guns, shooting pigeons and rabbits.

It didn't take me long to grow out of shooting animals though, something just told me it wasn't right, unless you had intensions of eating what you killed. Other weapons we would take to the old railway lines, were catapults and also arrows made from green garden canes.

We used playing cards folded in half for flights, and weighed the arrows at the front with pieces of chicken wire, and propelled by a shoe lace wrapped around the shaft of the arrow.

There were a few cottages dotted around and if we became thirsty we would knock on their doors and ask for a drink of water. The residents got used to us calling and some even gave us orange juice and biscuits.

The railway lines forked and one way led to Shortwood and the other way led to Rodway Common. Rodway has always been a place of interest for me. The Old Manor House situated at the top of Rodway Common holds a lot of history. Once occupied by Henry VIII's wife, Jane Seymour. The family coat of arms is still above the main doorway on the entrance.

Opposite on the common is the site of the annual travelling fairground that was held on bank holidays, a trend that has lasted for years. I loved the fairground there, it smelt of diesel oil from the generators and straw that was used on the ground should it get muddy and the music of Dave & Ansil Collins Double Barrel blasting out on the waltzers. The fairground workers always had weathered faces and were not always that friendly, so you did your best not to upset them. Some kids use to help out for a few pennies, but it didn't interest me.

My favorite attraction was Frankenstein's Castle. It was a small dark hallway with a cage in it and as you passed the cage you could just make out a figure at the back of it, and of course it was a man dressed up as the monster and he would jump out on you. I would go in there again and again. I loved the thrill of being scared, but was never fond of the rides as they made me feel sick. Even in a car I would have trouble with sickness so I stayed clear of the rides but kept face by liking Frankenstein's Castle.

Winning coconuts was easy, so when I got home I would hit a nail into the top of the coconut and drink the milk before cracking it open to eat.

After the fairground had left it was custom to go back to the site and look for money that had been dropped and lost by the crowds. Rodway Hill itself was covered by ferns and having grown there for hundreds of years, the ground was peaty and soft, so we would climb the fence at nearby Coxey's Wood Yard and steal sheets of hardboard. One side was smooth and the other course and we would take the boards to the top of the hill with the smooth side down and slide down it on the boards at some speed.

Another stop off place along the railway lines was The Bridge Inn in Shortwood, situated by an old abandoned coal yard. It was a great place to find lizards, and at nightfall you could see glow worms in the dark along the railway lines. The landlord's name was Maurice, he spoke very little and you always felt he didn't like kids much. He never smiled and he was expressionless.

It was a man's Inn, and its specialty was cider, the kind that still had bits of apple floating around in it. Inside were a few bar stools, the floor was stone and the seating away from the bar was made up of old bus seats long past their best. As kids, when we walked in it was like walking into a library. Just the wall clock ticking and old men with rosy cheeks and red noses playing cards or dominos.It was like an Inn from an old Hammer Horror film; but we were happy to sit outside sharing a bottle of lemonade on a summer's day.

Further up the road was a tip, which we loved. We would scale the fence and rummage through the rubbish, looking for pram wheels to make trolleys with or anything useful to us. We once found a box of iron on transfers and took them home to put on our T- shirts.

We were not aware of the dangers of course; either that or we didn't care. Failing to find any treasures, we would hunt the small ponds surrounding the tip for newts, salamanders, and grass snakes.

It's a shame to see the concrete jungle is now spreading into the countryside at an alarming rate. My youngest son didn't even believe me when I told him we used to catch lizards on the common; I don't think he has ever seen one in the wild.

Back in the suburbs Bonfire Night was a joyous occasion. My mates and I would walk around the local neighborhood knocking on people's doors and ask if they had any rubbish for the bonfire. This always brought a smile to the residents because it was a chance to get rid of maybe an old mattress they had in there garden or any old rubbish that was hanging around.

Old tyres were a favourite because they burned so well and old car seats, wardrobes, beds, and just about anything that would burn. You never knew what you would get and we would rummage through the bags of rubbish looking for any valuables and search the back of settees for money before we added it to the construction of the bonfire.

At night time you would guard the bonfire incase a rival gang tried to burn it down. We would sit around a fire cooking potatoes that we stole from the local allotment, in the ashes of the fire, sometimes playing cards or telling ghost stories. Even the local neighbors would keep an eye open for intruders trying to set fire to the bonfire. Every evening we would go home stinking of smoke and filthy dirty. By the time Bonfire Night came around our construction would be as high as a house.

It was a great time for unity and coalition between kids and adults and a great sense of community. Of course, you could never see this again in the modern world as councils introduced health and safety that ruled it out, along with other community things like the Whitson Monday Parade that took place in Kingswood High Street. The Whitson Monday Parade was a small scale carnival gathering of local churches, chapels and Sunday schools, that just about everyone in Kingswood would go to dressed in their Sunday best.

After the parade it was onwards to any of the many public houses in Kingswood with skittles and other games going on in their gardens, it was a time when your parents could sit back and enjoy a drink or two, it was a great gathering.

I agree that health and safety is necessary, but I'm a great believer in common sense and being allowed to think for yourself. In today's climate you can't even paint a front door without a method statement!

Another pastime was hedge hopping; first we would seek out a rank of houses that had privet hedges boundering the properties. We would tuck our trousers into our socks, so not to get them caught on anything, and then we would case our route carefully and find any obstructions that you might encounter, walking up and down the rank looking inconspicuous. Then from one end of the rank to the other, we would run and dive through the hedges, think the Grand National horse racing event! You had to save enough energy to escape the angry house owners who would chase you until they were out of steam; the object of the game was not to get caught because if you did you would get a slap around the listener! It was always a good idea to wear dark clothes and a hat covering as much of your identity as possible.

Imaginary tug of war was great fun as well. We would split up and half of our gang would go to one side of the road and the other half on the opposite side. New Cheltenham Road was a long stretch of tarmac that ran straight from top to bottom; we would play this game in a strategic place quarter of the way up by a big alley way for an escape route. In the 70's a car would come up or down the road every five or ten minutes. We would wait until it was dark and pretend there was a tug of war going on from one side of the road to the other, forcing the cars to stop, and then run like hell! Of course you couldn't do it now as a car comes up or down the road every five seconds!

A lot of the cars were made up of bits and pieces from the scrap yard; if your dad had a dent in his bonnet he wouldn't buy a new one, he would go to the scrap yard and purchase one off another car, regardless of the colour. It was very common to see cars like this.

We always seemed to be running away from someone. We were a ragamuffin lot, but there were some great characters in our neighborhood.

Charlie Jefferies was an old tramp like man who lived at the bottom of New Cheltenham Road. He wore a cap and long coat and his trousers were held up with string, but he was harmless and didn't bother anybody. His wife Blanche was an odd sort as well, she used to straddle over the drains in the road and urinate! I don't remember too much about her as she died leaving Charlie a widower.

I remember feeling upset when I heard he got broken into and beaten up. It came to light that someone thought the old guy had money, but to my knowledge he was poor and was always going around the streets picking up cigarette butts. I saw him the morning after he had been broken into picking up cigarette ends off the pavement, he had black eyes and cuts on his hands.

You could never really see into the man, his eyes were dark and lifeless, he seemed to look straight through you and his skin was weathered and like leather. I often thought of what hand he had been dealt with in life.

A few doors up from Charlie's house was a corner shop called Lloyds. It was the nearest shop to my house so I was often in there with a note from my mother to get supplies for the family.

Mr Lloyd was a quiet and trusting man and wore a doctors' like white coat. However, in the later teen years it didn't take long to find out that Mr Lloyd kept the potatoes in a back room of the shop in sacks, which was hard not to take advantage of in his absence while he was out there getting your potatoes that your mother had asked for in her note of supplies. No sooner was his back turned, I was leaning over the counter and helping myself to the sweet jars. Dishonest I know, but it was no good asking your mother for money, that's for sure. Money was hard to come by at the best of times, especially with seven mouths to feed. Your school uniform was paid for by weekly installments and on many occasions you were told to hide when the shop owner came to your door for his next installment. So, petty crime was a means to an end for us kids.

At the local post office and off license in New Cheltenham Road I would climb the fence at the back of the shop when it was dark and steal the empty cider bottles and take them to The Royal Archers Inn just around the corner to get a few pennies return money.

As the coming of the Supermarket dawned Mr Lloyd was forced to close down as were many other corner shops dotted around Kingswood.

John the butchers in nearby Holly Hill Road also shut down and I missed out on pocket money as these shops disappeared. John the butcher always wrapped your meat up in brown paper, but now my mother was coming home with meat wrapped in cellophane packaging from the supermarket.

You could feel the change coming, and most people don't like change and I'm no different for sure. The corner shops were small pillars in the community where everybody knew everybody in your neighborhood, and with the demise of the corner shop came a more unfamiliar feel with the local community.

Another character was a man we called Tele Gus. At the back of my house were garages and an allotment where we would dig a massive hole in the ground, and steal corrugated tin from Tele Gus's house, as his garden backed onto the allotment and his fence was made up of the tin and wood. We would put the tin over the hole and put the turf we had removed on top of the tin, so you would never know the den was there. We would sit in there for hours under candlelight, along with the worms and beetles. If Tele Gus caught you stealing his fence he would chase you for ages.

It was at the back of these garages that Tony Massey and I as infants once found some paint tins. We decided a Mini car that was parked there for some time could do with a lick of paint. We painted the car in all sorts of colours and made a real mess of it!

We hid in the long grass as the owner strolled down the garage ways; I could see the look of horror on his face as he saw the car, and this was no ordinary bloke! Dressed in Levi jeans, Doctor Martin shoes, and a half length black leather coat, everybody called him Al Capone. He was one of the toughest guys in the neighborhood, and he doesn't know to this day that it was Tony and I that did it. We really thought we were doing something good!

We were always getting up to something at the back of the garages or in my garden. At the back of my house there was an outhouse built on the side with a flat concrete roof.

We would often get up on the roof, but attached to it was also a greenhouse.

Now it had been drummed into me not to ever step on the green house when climbing onto the roof. Not only was it dangerous, but it was my father's pride and joy; he loved growing things in that old green house.

I'd given this advice to Tony, but one day as we were climbing up he put his foot onto the green house and fell right through it! He screamed and ran to the top of the garden, as a lane led from my house to his. I could see a horse shoe like cut in his leg, as we were both wearing shorts at the time; it flapped as he ran and I could see the bone, blood going everywhere!

My mum came out with her apron on and realising what had happened dragged me into the house, slapping me all the way.

"How many times have I told you, you stupid boy!" she *ranted.*

Tony nearly lost his leg from that; it has done him a bit of good though as he always told the girls the scar is from a shark bite!

In February 1972 all 289 coal miners' pits went on strike for a pay rise demanding £9.00 on top of their week's wages of £25.00. Picketing power stations, and rendering the country without electricity for up to nine hours a day. Now being only nine years old, I didn't really understand what was going on, only what I heard from my parents around the tea table. This was when most conversations came up, tea was at five o'clock on the dot; if you were late you didn't get a second chance, you would just have to go without tea, it was as simple as that. But I remember the strike as a great adventure that seemed, and in fact did last for weeks.

Each day my sisters, brother and myself would get a pep talk on the dangers of candles and the risk of fire before night fell. These strict orders were to be obeyed because my older sister Pamela had set her hair on fire with a candle under the bed in her junior years.

We would all retire to the living room as the light disappeared and light candles and huddle around the fireplace. We were lucky enough to have a good supply of coal that was delivered by an Afro Caribbean man called John, who lived in the small village called Pucklechurch. He was a big strong type, and wore a vest in all weathers covered in coal dust; it wasn't a job for the weak delivering coal in heavy sacks.

In the garden we had a coal shed, as did all the houses in our rank, and it was always kept well stocked.

Candles were the new household commodity, but during the blackouts they kept the fire services busy.

If one of us wanted the toilet we had to go in pairs, in case one of us dropped a candle and set the house on fire. It was the first time my family were all together for long periods of time, and conversations would go back to the Second World War and the air raids and blackouts back then. We would cook toast on the fire for supper on a long meat fork, and I used to imagine I was a cowboy in the wilderness sat there with my pretend guns on and cowboy hat.

I found it all very exciting, crawling around the living room scaring my sisters in the dimly lit room. Sometimes fearful, but safe in the protection of all my family; it was an adventure for me.

When the strike ended on 25th February 1972, I didn't feel happy the lights were back on, I felt saddened. I felt that things would just go back to normal and the unity I felt around my family would dissolve and disappear; I must have had insecurities.

The miners became amongst the highest paid working class. Strikes of all sorts were common ground in the 70's with the rise of Unions, and although sometimes inconvenient, I always admired people who would stand up and fight for something they thought to be right. I think this must be the anarchistic side of my personality.

The 70's also struck fear into children and adults alike in Bristol in December 1974. It was the lead up to Christmas and on 18th December at 7.30pm a man with an Irish accent makes a call to Bridewell Police Station in Bristol and explains there's a bomb in Park Street due to go off in the next twenty or thirty minutes. At 7.54pm a bomb explodes outside the Dixons photography shop. Then another bomb explodes in a bin at 8.30pm.

Only eight days earlier a bomb had gone off in Bath at the Corridors.

Terrorism by the IRA had come to the South West. It was something you saw on the news but thought it couldn't happen here, not where I live!

But for me the most terrifying thing of the time was the Cold War. I remember seeing a program on TV that explained what to do if there was a nuclear attack. The five minute warning, and how to make a barrier with bed mattresses. Now I'd seen what a nuclear war head was capable of and I for one wasn't buying it.

"Get behind a mattress? Who were they kidding?" I would sometimes lay awake in my bed and worry myself sick about it. I knew this threat was for real.

After the cold war ended in 1991 it came back to me just how real it was, when I found out that at the bottom of Hill Street, next to the Tenniscourt Inn in Kingswood, there was what I thought to be an electricity substation.

When it was demolished to make way for a block of flats, it came to light that in fact it was a nuclear bunker right on my doorstep!

In the summer of 1976 it was the hottest on record. We spent the mornings at Glen Briton's house in the summer holidays, as his mother, father and brother Colin all worked.

Glen had a nice house across the road from me; we would watch Sesame Street, The Double Deckers and The Flashing Blade on TV, then play some of his brother's records that mostly consisted of Queen and Status Quo. Colin played the guitar and we would strap his guitar on and pretend to play it along with the record, posing in the window for passersby to see.

Failing going to Glen's we would go to Mike Wilson's house just up the road. Mike had a brother Nigel and a sister

Jane, of whom we wouldn't let, play with us because she was a girl.

Across the road from him lived an unfortunate kid that we used to call Gronk. The poor bugger always had snot running down his face and was always filthy dirty and never seemed to have his coat on properly, it was always kind of hanging off his shoulders, but because he lived in our neighborhood nobody ever bothered him.

There was also a rather large woman who would walk to the shops every day at around 11.00am passing Mike's house. When we saw her coming we would hang our feet out of the window wagging them like a dying fly, and shouting 'Fatty Piggy' at her; God knows why but we found it funny at the time.

Four doors down from Mike's house a terror lay in wait for us and it came in the form of a large black dog we called Keyda Kai. It was the dog that all your nightmares were made of. The big black monster would lay in the garden waiting for passersby and it would go ballistic, growling and frothing at the mouth. If he wasn't chained up you had to run for your life because Keyda Kai took no prisoners. Of course being kids we did tend to tease it a little; it was good fun having a wild dog chase you around.

We had our own football team in that summer of 76, Glen Britton, Martin Barnard, Chunky Williams, Mike Wilson, Steve Pusey, Jerry Bowden, myself and a few others, and our manager was my now brother in-law Eddy Pillinger, married to my sister Pam. We named the team Stanton Albion, after the place we used to practice in Stanton Close. No goal posts or nets, just the side of a garage as the goal mouth. We didn't have kits or anything, and just played rival gang football teams from time to time.

I could never forget that glorious summer of 76, waiting for Joe's Ice-cream van on an evening to get a plastic cone filled with ice-cream with a bubble gum at the bottom of it, or a cider ice lolly. At the end of the night we would all sit on Jerry Bowden's wall on the corner of Stanton Close and opposite my house in New Cheltenham Road, and wait for the cry of our mothers shouting at us to come home as it's getting dark. So one by one we would disappear home.

That summer seemed to last forever, and I wish it did!

Outside 260 New Cheltenham Road 1968

1967, in awe of Father Christmas

CHAPTER - 3 YOUTH YOUTH YOUTH.

In the 70's and 80's there were youth clubs springing up all over the country. Within one mile of where I lived in New Cheltenham Road, there were three. The Made Forever, The Summit, and The YMCA. Each youth club was a little different to the other.

The Made Forever, was a small shabby tin like hut situated at the bottom of Anchor Road in Kingswood. Being at that end of town, it would attract a rougher bunch of kids. But it was very good if you liked music, as you could choose what you would like to listen to by asking the youth leader what to purchase on his next visit to the record shop.

Most evenings at the club were spent playing cards for some pennies, or listening to music, or darts or table tennis. Not much else was on offer, but it was somewhere to hang out with your mates and try it on with some local girls. The club's leader was a gentleman called Neil; he was a Welshman, who was tall in stature with a slightly receding hair line and walked like he had springs on his feet. Neil was an all round good guy, and definitely had some influence on me.

Keeping the kids off the street was the main objective of the youth leader, and once a year at The Made Forever there was a national club week. Of course, they were never short of volunteers, because your objective was to collect money from the public in money tins provided by the club. The tins unscrewed half way down, but were protected by a sticker around the join to stop you taking money out. So you were given your tin, and stickers to give to anyone who donated.

Off we would set to the shopping area of Kingswood, shaking our tins at just about anyone passing, hanging around the once mighty Woolworths shop doors in the high street, and also asking in public houses, coffee shops, on buses, and just about everywhere we could think of. Our enthusiasm was spurred on by knowing that we could get money out of the tins without the youth leader finding out.

We did this by using a small pen knife inserted into the money slot, then we tipped the tin up and down until, eventually, coins would slide down the knife into your hand. Everybody was happy on national club week, the club got money, and the kids had a small share in it also and no real harm was done; after all it was for the kids benefit.

The youth club offered everything you would expect in the 70's and early 80's. New recruits would come and go, and on the occasion, fights would be arranged in the small lane that led to the club doors. The Made Forever had a fenced grass area outside, which we used as our football pitch and used our jumpers for goal posts when the club was not open. The girls stayed in their gang and the boys stayed in theirs. It was a small world I seemed to live in, everybody knew everybody else in the area and everyone had respect for your mate's parents.

One of the helpers at the Made Forever was a guy called Pete. Now Pete had an unfortunate car accident one night, and his injuries were far from okay; he suffered some back and head injuries. I didn't take much notice of him before the accident, he was just another guy who helped out at the club from time to time, but when he eventually came out of hospital he had a metal frame around the top half of his body and neck, which you couldn't help noticing. He still helped out at the club, but his personality completely changed. Pete was a big bloke and strong as an ox, the problem was that after the accident he didn't know his own strength and would grab you by the arm and squeeze the life out of it. Everyone was weary of Pete; you would cross the road if you saw him, you just didn't know what he was going to do next, he was very unpredictable.

One afternoon we were playing football, and Pete took it upon himself to referee the game. Half way through the match a girl walked across the pitch and Pete grabbed her, turned her upside down, and dangled her by her ankle! He was bloody scary at times.

On winter evenings waiting for the club to open, we would gather around the heating ventilation pipes warming our hands from the hot carbon spilling out into the atmosphere, and you would try your best not to inhale any of the fumes. Inside the club was a large dance hall, which nobody went on until the lights were turned off, then it would gradually fill up with kids, and all the boys stood with their backs to the wall like wallflowers, whilst the girls danced away to the disco music; that was until someone asked for a punk song and then the girls would leave!

The other club, The Summit, was next to Kingswood Park and it was a different sort of club to the Made Forever. I never really liked it; it was for the type of kids who liked disco music. It was almost like a night club, and to this day I've never been fond of such dwellings. The Summit was more up market than the Made Forever.

The only memories I have of that club that stick in my mind as a teenager, was of a girl that was constantly taken advantage of at the back of the club. I felt sorry for her, she craved attention and, if my memory serves me right, she had some parenting problems, it was all very sad.

Having said that, I remember a helper there whose name was Dianne, and she was all for the kids and I admired that.

The YMCA, next to the onion factory in Kingswood, was a great little club. The facilities were good, and it had a pinball machine in the lounge and a pool table and dart board. It was at that club that I first heard The Stranglers, Blondie and Elvis Costello.

Upstairs were rooms you could hang out in, and it was in one of these rooms that a funny thing happened one summers evening. For some strange reason a good mate of mine, who I will call Dan, decided he would take a dare and shit out of the window. Directly below the window was the club office, and I volunteered to go and make sure the youth leader, a Yorkshire man called Eric who had a bald head and a big round face, was not in the office before the dare could take place.

Dan got into position, dropped his trousers and hung his backside out of the old metal casement window and wrapped the curtain around his body, as not to reveal himself. So I made my way down the stairs and into the office. Eric, the youth leader, was sat at his desk talking to a lady who was a helper, she was called Margret. *"What can we do for you?"* Eric asked. I didn't expect anyone to be in the office, so I stumbled my words, and asked for a table tennis bat. With that there was a 'splatting' noise on the office window, and Eric and Margret looked on with their mouths wide open in disbelief to see excrement running down the window! I ran out in fits of laughter, and Eric pushed past me, running up the stairs and I followed.

There were about six in the room, including Dan, and Eric was red faced, shouting, *"OWN UP OR I WILL SHUT THE CLUB DOWN!"* At this moment, I noticed Dan had wiped his bottom in the curtains, and by this time I was crying with laughter! Eric threatened to call the police, so Dan owned up and Eric made him take the curtains home to wash. Dan just threw them in a lane by his house, and after a downpour of rain, that was a good enough wash, and took them back; his excuse was he just couldn't get to the toilets in time! It still remains one of the funniest things I've ever seen.

Eric was a nice bloke really, and he even took us fishing from time to time.

Both the YMCA and The Summit have now made way for housing, the Made Forever was knocked down and rebuilt and still remains a youth club to this day.

So, what was there to do when the youth club wasn't open? Well, in general, nothing! Although, we did have a few strategically placed areas to hang out.

One was at the bottom of my street, where there was a phone booth just up from the Anchor Inn. It was always good to hang around a phone booth in case you needed to call your friends up for something. The calls would cost two pennies for three minutes. Phone booths were not nice to make calls really, they always stank of urine.

So, sitting on the wall by the phone booth, no matter what the weather, was always a good meeting place, it was better to meet that way instead of calling for your mates, and risking getting told to piss off by their father.

To amuse ourselves we would watch for cars going by, looking at the number plates of the vehicles. It was a game we played, first you would have to spot a number one on a number plate, then look for a number two, and so on. I think I got up to around one hundred and fifty before I gave up the ghost. It was a daft game, but it culled the boredom.

In between looking for number plates, if someone wanted to fart everyone would get really excited. Cry's of, "*I got one coming*," would echo down the street, and whoever indeed had to let a fart go would lay on their back with their legs in the air, waiting for one of us to ignite the fart with a match or lighter. Who ever made the biggest flame was the hero of the hour.

Sometimes, in the winter months, it was freezing sat on that wall, but no matter what the weather it was still better to be with your mates than sat at home bored. If it was raining we would find an empty council garage at the back of my house, and sit in there with candles, playing cards. Apart from the youth club there was absolutely nothing to do in the evening, especially in the winter months.

Kids hanging around on street corners sometimes seemed to bother the older generation of the time, and sometimes you would get remarks from them like, "*You lot should be in the bloody army*" or, "*Why don't you lot piss off home*," We never took any offence, we respected our elders, it was how we were all brought up.

We had nick names for most of them; Harry Hobnail, because he always wore hobnail boots; The Vest Man, because this guy always wore a vest out, no matter what the weather; Queeny, who was a short little lady and wore a head scarf and mackintosh and wasn't quite the sharpest tool in the box; One Arm Bandit; Tornado; we had names for all of them in our area.

When I look back I can't complain too much about my youth, in fact a small part of me feels rather sorry for youth these days. Tuning on my radio just the other day, I stumbled on a discussion about the so called lads magazines, and if the covers with scantily dressed women on the front, were unsavory to been seen in newsagents shops by minors? I'm thinking the lucky buggers don't know they are born; I had to make do with my mother's mail order catalogue and look at the women's underwear section to get my kicks as a lad.

The age old question soon raised its head that, are these magazines derogative to women? So, I thought about it for a fraction of a second, and of course came up with the answer, no! There's nothing unsavory about a beautiful women's body is there? What I mean is, our girlfriends and wives don't spend hours getting ready in front of the mirror to look bad do they! All sorts of people were picking up the phone and calling in to the radio to have their say; one woman even called it prostitution?

I thought to myself, we are all prostitutes; we all do something for money? And most of us don't like what we do! I'm sat there in my chair, thinking to myself, 'For god's sake, if you don't like lads magazines, don't buy them!' I don't like peanut butter, but it's not going to upset me if my local store sells it!

One thing is for sure, as a youth in the 70's and 80's, I had a certain amount of freedom. Free from moaning busybodies, who seem to have nothing better to do than scare the youth half to death with what could happen to them if they read a lads magazine or stay on a video games too long.

I might well be wrong, but in my opinion, we should let kids grow up, it's a natural metamorphism, your feathers are young, but you will learn to fly!

In some ways, I think of my youth in comparison with Oliver Twist, there are some very poignant scenes in that great story. The scene when Oliver has a fight at the Undertakers with the older boy who works there and Mr. Bumble is called to help. Mr. Bumble turns to the Undertaker's wife and says, *"The problem is mam, you're giving the boy too much meat!"* And, of course, the most famous scene when Oliver asks, *"Please sir, can I have some more?"*

Think about it?

CHAPTER 4 – MAN -V- ELEPHANT

Confused and with no direction, I left school early with no exams. I've not much more to say about school life in the 80's other than, and nothing less than - child abuse! I've always had a problem with the education system in the UK. In private school they teach kids the more beneficial learning, so why can't they teach the same in secondary schools? Well I guess secondary education is for the foot soldiers and private school is the future Generals. It's all very black and white to me.

It was a small wonder that football violence was at its high in the 70's, the abused became the abuser. I spent a good few years in factory life; you kind of become institutionalised in that environment, and it's safe and you're in your comfort zone.

It wasn't until my father Ernie died that I thought it was time to leave. I respected him very much and it was my father who got me the job in the first place, after working in a warehouse for a builder's merchant. Perhaps that was the reason I stayed there when he was alive?

My dad Ernie was a small framed man; he was a light weight in the boxing divisions, to give you some idea. I can only describe Ernie as a spiv, a commonly known word used during the Second World War; it describes as a petty criminal smartly dressed man selling black market goods at a profit.

He was never without a roll of cash in his pocket, he was as cunning as a fox and as slippery as a snake, but he knew how to make money and all seven of his children never went without.

I remember a time when on one Saturday morning he told me to go with him and he showed me how to make some easy money. We left the house and headed for the local supermarket in Kingswood High Street. He bought lots of packets of mushrooms and we headed back home.

Back at the house he retrieved a wicker basket from the shed in the garden, filled it with straw and moss and took the mushrooms from the plastic packaging and placed them in the wicker basket.

"*Now let's make some money*," he said to me.

We walked to the Anchor Inn at the bottom of New Cheltenham Road; it was one of his favorite Inns. As we walked into the bar, Ernie shouted, "*Me and the boy have been picking fresh mushrooms this morning. Who wants the best mushrooms money can buy?*"

Within minutes there was a queue of men scrabbling to get their hands on what they thought was organic mushrooms, freshly picked in the early morning due, and of course these come at a higher price than the ones you got at a supermarket!

My father spent more time at The Anchor Inn than he did at home. Either that or he could be found at The Horseshoe Inn on Siston Common; it was a stone's throw from the Anchor.

Leaving The Horseshoe one night he was knocked down by a car. He had obviously had a few to drink and didn't see the car coming and it was probably best he was drunk, as he said he didn't feel a thing. He was out of work for some time though with injuries to his chest and head.

When I was in my late teens I would walk to The Horseshoe Inn with him every Sunday; the Inn opened at twelve noon and shut again at 2 o'clock. I would sit around the table with his friends; a colourful lot they were, always planning how to make the next pound or two.

One of my father's friends I liked was a man called Des. He was short in stature and had tight curly hair and always dressed immaculate. He would greet me with kind words every time I saw him and always got me a drink.

Later down the line he got divorced from his wife who was a lot younger than him and they had one child together, an albino child. After he got divorced he never seemed the same. The smartly dressed man I had once known had become scruffy in appearance and looked withdrawn. As I understand it Des had always been on some kind of medication and when his marriage broke up he stopped taking it. The poor guy just went from bad to worse, and eventually became homeless.

I would see him up the common on the old railway lines dressed in a bright yellow track suit, some of the kids would call out 'banana man' when they saw him, and he pushed a bicycle along with him with carrier bags tied to the handle bars. He had totally given up.

It wasn't long before I got news that he had been found dead up on the railway lines. I felt very sorry for him, and the guy wouldn't have hurt a fly. The last time I had spoken to him was at the dole office. I didn't really know what to say to him as he sat next to me. I just came out with, *"Where do you drink now then Des?"*

He replied, *"I can't drink anymore, the cold will get me if I do and I will die."*

My mother used to send me to The Anchor Inn on an evening to fetch her a bag of salted peanuts and a bottle of stout. I didn't mind this, as I would take the empty bottles back and get a penny for each one I returned.

The landlord of the Anchor was a man called Billy Bat. He was a slim bald headed man with a loud voice.

His second in command was a man I used to call Sharky because he had teeth like a shark, all sharp and jagged; he had strawberry blond hair and a barrel chest and a big red face.

As you walked into The Anchor Inn, there was a door to your right, which was the lounge, a place for couples and ladies, and a door on your left which was the bar. Straight in front of you was a door that led to a small little room about a meter square were you could buy pies, pasties, and beer etc. without going into the pub itself. My mother used to call it the 'bottle and jug'.

Every time I went there for my mother, Sharky would say, *"What do you want me cock?"*

I would reply the usual, *"One bottle of stout and a packet of nuts."*

One day I went for my mother and as usual Sharky said, *"What do you want me cock?"*

I replied, *"No thanks, just a bottle of stout and a packet of nuts."*

Sharky chased me out of the pub shouting, *"I will hammer you in the floor like a carpet tack!"* I had to explain to my mother that they had ran out of stout and nuts on that day!

Sharky went home one night and fell in the fire burning his eye, it looked awful. My brother from then on called him 'snot eye'.

My brother John used to frequent the Anchor a lot as well, until one night he super glued all the glasses to the bar and tables and Billy Bat banned him for life. My brother John made up a rhyme he would shout out every time he walked past the pub. He would shout at the top of his voice;

"Billy Bat had a shit on the kitchen floor, Mrs Bat cleaned it up and Billy done some more!"

He had a wicked sense of humor.

I was never very fond of the Anchor Inn, I guess it was because my father was always in there and it would upset my mother when he would come in late shouting and moaning and waking everyone up.

Some nights I would lay in bed unable to sleep waiting for the sound of the back door to open and my father to come in drunk, not knowing if I was going to hear an argument or not between him and my mother. It scared me a lot, and my heart would beat twenty to the dozen on hearing the back door open on his arrival home. I knew if he was out late the chances are there would be an argument. It terrified me. I would put the pillow over my head and try to think of something else. It was something you didn't talk about with your mates; you didn't want anyone to know what went on in your house.

The next day after an argument I would hear my mother saying, *"That's it I'm bloody leaving him!"* The thought of that also terrified me; I've never been the one for change, I just don't like it.

On a Sunday afternoon he would go to bed after he had been to the pub, and if you woke him all hell would break loose. So you had to sneak around the house as quiet as possible. He would have the electric blanket turned on just before he went to bed on a Sunday. One Sunday my mother forgot to turn it off and Ernie came staggering out of the bedroom in a right mess saying, *"She is trying to kill me!"* We all found it very funny indeed; it was a bit of karma.

My father would say the public house is where he did business.

I didn't like Sundays very much, as it was back to school the next day and it was bath day! It's funny looking back, but I knew what day it was by what I had for tea or dinner. Sunday was of course a roast; Monday was bubble and squeak, that was made from the left over's from Sunday; Tuesday was liver and onions; Wednesday was egg and chips; Thursday was a surprise meal, and of course Friday fish and sandwiches on Saturday. I recently cleared a drawer out in my kitchen and found thirty two take away menus!

Nowadays you don't even have to cook if you don't want to; in fact you don't have to leave the house! Life is fast these days, and there's not that much time for cooking for the modern woman or man.

At Christmas there were always boxes of toys and sweets piled high in our hallway that my father Ernie was selling. It was very exciting as a child to see all these goods stacked in the house, and if it was sweets we always got a box for ourselves. Being curious, when I asked him where it all came from, he would say, *"It fell off the back of a lorry."* I actually believed that was the case!

My father Ernie was way before his time, being an avid horse racing fan he devised what we know now, as race night or virtual racing. He would make up horse racing names and take the role as a horse racing commentator and record it on an old reel to reel tape recorder. Everyone would buy a horse in the race and only Ernie would know the winner; of course he couldn't lose. He set the odds from the off, so it would always be a winner with not very good odds that won. He was the type of man that could sell sand to an Arab!

I respected him, he only ever hit me once as a child, and that was when I snapped his split cane fishing rod, playing around in the shed. He chased me all around the garden until he caught me, and then he took his belt off and gave me a good whacking.

He loved his greyhounds and would spend pounds and pounds on their upkeep. Some he kept in the shed and we were not allowed to pet them in any way. On the morning of a grey hound race he would never give the dogs water, so not to bloat them, but on some occasions my mother Iris would give them a sneaky drink. If Ernie found out he would be furious.

The last time I saw him was while he was in hospital, he looked frail and weak, and pumped full of morphine, he was jabbering somewhat, not making much sense at all. I asked him if he really did see the Devil. It was a story he told us when we were young.

When he lived in Wales, a fight had broken out in the street, and his parents had told him to stay in bed, but being curious he wanted to see what was going on. As he got to the top of the stairs from his bedroom he said the Devil was at the bottom looking up at him. He said he had a rag like face and curled up toes.

He replied, *"Yes, I did see the Devil!"*

He also said, *"I remember when you called me a bald headed bastard."* This hurt me. It was something I had said many years previous in a heated argument about a bet he put on for me for West Ham United to win the FA cup in 1980 and of course they did.

The winnings were £17.00, a small fortune in the 80's, but I never did see any of the money.

`I fought back the tears at the hospital, I didn't want him to see me cry, and he would have called me a sissy for that. In those days you didn't get the hugs or kisses you get in family life today, it was all very proper. The only times you would get a hug would be at a family party or event or when the beer was flowing some.

He was unwell for some time with cancer. I remember sat on a wall by The Anchor Inn one afternoon and noticed my brother's car coming around the roundabout with my mother in the front seat and my father Ernie in the back, they had been to the hospital. They didn't see me, but as I looked at my father in the back of the car I could tell it was not good news, he was just starring in open space and he looked very withdrawn. I knew from that day what was to become of him and it's for that reason I've never forgot seeing him in the back of my brother's car that day.

It's funny because in the last year of his life he stopped going to the Anchor Inn, and all the bickering stopped. It was nice to see my parents happy at long last, and at the grand old age of 62 he finally settled down.

I learnt of his death from his friend who he worked with at the factory (Bendix Weston House).

"What are you doing here today?" asked his mate Bob as I was sat at my bench. He looked puzzled?

Bob was a good friend of Ernie's; they worked together in the machine shop in the factory.

"Well perhaps it's the best thing to just get on with it." he said. Now I looked puzzled.

"What the hell are you going on about bob?" I asked him.

"I'm so sorry to hear about Ernie." he replied. He had seen my mother on his way to work and got the news. I knew what he meant then. I stood up and headed for the door. I didn't even tell the foreman I was leaving. I had one thing on my mind, to get to my mother's house. I knew what had happened straight away. I was in shock.

"Got to get home, got to get home." I kept saying to myself. Then I felt anger. Why had my family not told me? Why did I have to hear the news from his friend? Maybe I was looking for someone to blame. Maybe my family were

trying to protect me. But I was going to find out sooner or later wasn't I!

My brother John and my then brother in-law Clive were at his bedside when he passed away. This cut deep in me.

It took me a long time to forgive and forget, and it haunted me for years as I felt like an outsider, a black sheep. I didn't even get to go in the funeral car on the day. Instead I was bundled into my brother in-law's car. I didn't speak a word on the way to the church, and it felt like I wasn't part of my family. I couldn't say anything to anybody as I didn't want to upset my mother, so I just went along with it.

The death of my father had a huge impact on me, it really did change me. He wasn't the sort of dad that you could say, *"Hey dad, I love you."* You just didn't feel you could say anything like that to him. He would have probably laughed.

I remember not long after his death, standing at my bench in the factory and looking up at the florescent lighting that covered the factory ceilings, and thinking there must be more to life than this place?

In India they train an elephant from a very young age. They drive a stake into the ground and chain the elephant to it. The young elephant is not strong enough to pull the stake from the ground, and it goes back and forth trying to free itself, until eventually it gives up. When the elephant is an adult and collecting honey in the jungle, its owners take him back to the same stake after a day's work. The elephant, now an adult, could easily pull the stake from the ground, but doesn't as it's bred in him and he is institutionalised and he won't free himself.

Was I to be that elephant? No, not that day I wasn't! I headed for the factory door for the last time. If I had to work it was going to be doing something I didn't mind doing with people who were in some way or another on the same wave length as me.

My first port of call was a job with my mate Rob Ryall for his dad Dennis as a painter. My teacher was Rob's older brother Terry. Now Terry is the kind of guy who is a perfectionist; it took two years before he would let me paint a door!!

We worked a lot in St Paul's in Bristol during and after the St Paul's riots. The riots were the first of its time and spread across the country in 1984.

St Paul's was a deprived area and had all the problems you would expect; drugs, violence and prostitution etc. The obvious answer to the government was to throw money at it, and so we worked there for many years. Even the guy who we subcontracted off had to pay protection money; if he didn't they would get in the property overnight and smash the place up. The majority of the people were friendly but there were an element of bad ones too.

One evening we were ready to leave and a guy called Marcus, who worked with us, couldn't find where he had parked his motorbike. Then we heard a shout from one of the workers who had just left. He shouted up the road, *"Marcus your motorbike is down here!"*

When we went to take a look, the bike was smoldering. It had been caught on fire. Poor old Marcus cried; it was his pride and joy!

The problem we had is that when the police raided anywhere, they would come in the disguise of builders.

Many times we were called 'pig's', 'coppers', 'C.I.D', and 'blood clots'.

One summers' evening we were getting ready to go home and we noticed some activity out in the street. There were cars pulling up at each end to block any other cars coming down the road. Two cars pulled up outside the house we were working in, and one guy jumped out of the car wielding a large knife that he was now tapping on the gate of the house we were in and looking straight at us. It was obvious something was going down, so a quick hand gesture to the guy with the knife just to let him know we have not seen anything and we retreated back into the house and closed the door.

Within ten minutes the cars pull off and the street returned to normal, so we then left. It was nothing out of the ordinary in those days.

In the same street we had smelt something horrible for days. Trying to find out what the hell it was we looked through a window of a house on the opposite side of the road and saw some poor guy dead in his living room; he must have been there for ages.

There was also a women who lived at the top of the street who would often walk around in the morning stark naked without a care in the world; obviously high on drugs.There was never a dull moment.

I had many experiences in St Paul's. One day I was working in a hostel; they gave food packages to the needy every day at 2.00pm. Queues of waifs and strays would line up; the place had security locks everywhere.

So one afternoon I was taking a break and as I looked up City Road I saw a guy staggering down the street. He was about six foot away from me and then he collapsed in a heap on the floor. He was green! His eyes were rolling, and he was frothing at the mouth. I noticed a syringe hanging out of his arm; he was overdosing on heroine. Now for a split second it did pass my mind whether to just leave him, I knew this guy was going to cause a lot of heartache and grief to a lot of people in the future, but being human I rang the ambulance services.

I explained the guy was overdosing, and the person on the other end of the phone asked me how I knew this? I told him he had a needle hanging out of his arm.

"Can you please remove the needle from his arm." he asked me.

"You got more chance of England winning the World Cup mate." I told him. The ambulance came within minutes. The paramedics worked on the guy and put him into the back of the ambulance and sped off.

Within a few days I saw the same guy in new clothes, shoes, and baseball hat staggering down the road on another planet!

You had to have your wits about you in those days. When working in some of the buildings you could come across syringes anywhere, they could be taped underneath the stairs handrails, or on the top of door frames; just about anywhere concealed, you had to be very careful indeed.

I once asked a heroin addict what made him get hooked. He told me it was like a ten minute orgasm! Now that has got to be a hard habit to kick I thought to myself, so best stay clear of that shit!

I felt sorry for the people lining up to get basic foods, eggs, bread, beans and milk.

I once worked at Marks & Sparks, and they would give their leftover and out of date food to pig farmers for pigs to eat. Why, when there are people near to starving makes me feel sick. Let's get one thing straight; there's enough food to go around!

Of course the only thing I was interested in was getting home after a day's work, have a bath, eat my tea and out the door to the Kings Arms in Kingswood. I was always in a rush to get out. Now one night I got home, and as quick as I could I took off my t-shirt and work trousers and pants at the same time. Unbeknown to me my pants were still in the trouser leg of my work trousers. I went out and got drunk, chatted a load of nonsense, curry and chips on the way home and then bed. Nothing out of the ordinary.

The next day Terry was sounding the van horn. I'm late; again! Quickly pulling my trousers on I rushed out of the door. Now we used to stop at an Indian shop in Eastville called Dewannas to get our newspapers and drink etc. I was wandering about the busy shop looking for something to help my sore head. Rob said me from across the shop, *"Louie, Louie, look down!"* He was now laughing and so was Terry?

Now I was still half drunk and I eventually looked down to my feet, and saw my pants that I'd worn the day before around one of my ankles; they must have still been in my trouser leg from the day before and in my haste to get out the door before Terry drove off without me, I'd not noticed this. By this time the shop keeper thought something was going on. He saw me bend down, pick something up and put it in my pocket.

"What you putting in pocket?" He shouted in his Indian accent, across the shop.

I ignored him and now the other people in the shop were all looking at me and Terry and Rob walked the other way as if to say, *"We have nothing to do with him!"*

"What you put in pocket? I call police!" the shop keeper shouted.

I reply, *"My pants!"*

Now Terry and Rob were in fits of laughter, and I had to go to the counter and explain in front of all of the customers that my pants must have been stuck in my trouser leg from the day before. I left the shop to silenced customers and a wide opened mouth shop keeper!

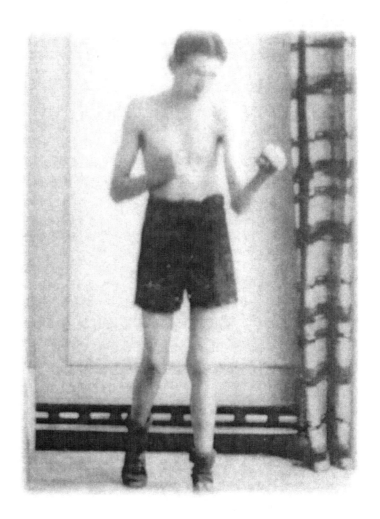

A young Ernie Lewis in boxing stance

1980's St Paul's Riots

CHAPTER 5 – I KNOW NOTHING

The great Greek philosopher Socrates once quoted, *"I am the wisest man in the world, because I know I know nothing."*

Poor old Socrates, one of the world's greatest philosophers was put to death in 399BC in Athens for charges of corrupting the young and impiety.

It gives us food for thought, what does the average person really know? The answer is, of course, nothing.

But In our small world, our tiny bubble, we are aware of the grip tightening on our societies, closing in on us like a dark cloud from a mythical story. Our fascination with voyeurism, we are constantly being watched, and we are constantly watching. Our thirst for encroaching on other people's lives is somewhat fascinating.

In most countries now, you are monitored every single day of your life. It's almost as if we need looking after, because we sometimes make wrong decisions, we cannot be trusted. It paints a picture of a super being looking over us, a god like figure, with technology at his fingertips. The oppression we sometimes feel is, at times, unbearable - so a well earned holiday abroad is in need, for escapism.

For me, a holiday abroad is not about where water meets dirt, it's about feeling a sense of freedom, to go to countries that are a little behind our own country, in structure of societies. For us, it's bliss not to have so many rules and regulations to abide by. So have we come too far to quick?

As a child growing up, I hated holidays, I would have rather been with my friends, and everything was simple, just like when you go on holiday now. I'm always watchful on my adventures abroad, and let's be honest, when you're on a plane flight there's not much more to do than observe other people.

I notice the ever changing fashions that come in and out year after year. Being born in the early 60's, I've witnessed some weird and wonderful fashion changes.

I first became aware of fashion when I started senior school in 1974. It was the birth of the crimplene trousers that first caught my attention. Made from polyester and patch pockets and high waste buttons, the higher the waist band the better, so, at times, they would nearly reach your chest! The problem with polyester crimplene trousers was that they were highly inflammable, so they disappeared off the shelves as fast as they appeared!

To compliment your high waste patch pocket trousers, came the introduction of the stack shoe, a fashion helped along by the glam rock era, and of course the higher the shoe the better.

So, to round up this first fashion faze of mine, I had pockets on the side of my trousers I could not reach, a waist band so high it gave you indigestion, and shoes that I could barely walk in!

Footwear was always important as a teenager, in the 70's there were many trends. The Moccasin shoes, which were made of leather and resembled a red Indian style shoe. The brogue shoes, that were a sensible choice, with their leather soles; apart from when you upgraded your brogues by purchasing some blakeys and nailed them to the soles, which made the shoes sound like a tap dancer when walking along, but also made them slippery as hell! The birth of the Doctor Martin boots and shoes, and your status was measured by how many lace holes you had in your boots. Some had so many they would nearly reach your knees, resembling a Roman soldier! On the down side of the trend was the much cheaper version we called Major doemoes. These were rejects from the boot factory, and were seen as un-cool if you had a pair. And, of course, a favorite of mine was the monkey boot.

Not all fashions and trends disappear into obscurity. The Doctor Martin boots are as popular today as when they first arrived on the scene; also other brands like the Fred Perry shirts, the Harrington jacket, and of course not forgetting the biker's leather jacket.

Some fashions have longevity, but most don't. They come, they go, but practicality will always prevail.

Just take a look at a 1980's fashion, the shell suit, yet in its day it was seen as pretty cool to be seen in. Today's fashion of wearing your jeans so far down your waist that the crotch ends up by your knees, will have the same longevity as the shell suit. To be brutally honest, I've never been much of a fashion follower; it could be that if you put me in a twenty thousand pound suit, I would still look like a bag of shit tied up.

Einstein had it all worked out, he would buy, let's say ten of the same suits, shirts, and shoes, and that way he didn't have to think about what he was going to wear when he went out, freeing his mind to concentrate on more important things.

Vulgarity always seems to be in fashion, just take a look at any fashion show on TV, most of the models look like they could do with a good meal. Having said all that, there's nothing like a bit of shopping therapy to make us feel good.

A lot of fashions and trends are influenced by what we watch on TV, right down to how we decorate our homes. The lava lamp has lasted for decades, and art deco has always been a front runner. The old TV series, Starsky and Hutch made knitted coats a fashion statement in the 70's, and of course, the mullet hair style came mainly from TV.

Pop stars also provoke fashion statements. Take the Beatles' haircuts in the 60's; The Bay City Rollers' tartan fashion; David Bowie feather haircuts; glam rock, punk rock, hip hop, disco; the list goes on and on.

We use fashion to express ourselves, to give a public image of what we are like as a person, how we want to be viewed by the public. If you wear a twenty thousand pound suit, you want everyone to know it's expensive. For me, if you pay, you get what you deserve, or on the flip side, you get what you pay for…

This is sometimes true when you enter a bargain shop; they are pretty easy to recognize, with giveaway names, like, The Bargain House, or Everything For A Pound, or something along those lines. We have all been victims of these outlets, thinking you're getting a bargain and value for money when you buy a bin liner full of cornflakes, only to find when you get them home they taste like petrol!

I swear to god if I opened a shop called A Load of Crap, people would come flocking in like lemmings. The buy one get one free culture? Let's get one thing straight, nothing is for free!

I recently had a two for one meal at a local public house, I ordered the giant fish and chips meal, only to find that I have seen more fish in a fish finger!

I find it fascinating that hoards of people will camp out on the streets to get to the front of a queue, to the latest big store sale, to buy last year's fashion that didn't sell well in the first place; the mind boggles?

Of course, the down side to the ever changing fashions is that it has made us into a throw away culture. Everything from clothes, TVs, fridges, to mobile phones ends up in the bin. We all want the latest model, rendering rubbish tips and land fill spiraling out of control. I was horrified to hear that much of our plastic waste gets sent off to India; no disrespect meant, but the last time I looked they had enough crap of their own! So it's official, there's a lot of crap going on these days!

Having said that, practicality usually gives a fashion or trend longevity, this cannot always be the case, and a fashion can be resurrected at any given time, and certain objects can go on to be iconic.

Take the Raleigh Chopper bicycle from the 1970's. These not so practical bicycles, with their small front wheel and large back wheel and ape hanger handle bars loosely modeled on the Hells Angels chopper motor bikes, were unstable at best. Yet they have become very collectable and iconic to the era. It also had a junior model called The Chipper. The Chopper bike was the must have bicycle of the 1970's, and on every boy or girls' Christmas wish list.

Christmas always produces a trend and must have item. Some have immense longevity, like The Scalelectrix car racing track, and Subbuteo football game, to name a few.

As older adults, we like to re-live our youth through our own children and so, we keep on buying these products. Subbuteo is still played, despite the advanced video games of today, although it's mostly played by adults.

Of course, anything can become collectable as time passes. The Cabbage Patch Dolls, which were introduced in 1983, caused chaos at the shops as the must have Christmas toy and are now collectable. Mr. Potato Head, introduced in 1952, is to this day, still selling.

As time goes by the video game consoles will have their day again in the future. The now fashionable drink of Cider, once a drink for alcoholics who couldn't afford real beer, was then, and still is, cheaply produced, has for some strange reason, become the drink to be seen with. Roll your own cigarettes are now more popular than ever before, but I think that's due to the tax on tailor made ones to be honest.

Fashion and trends are like a rollercoaster, the question is, when do you get off? But, what do I know? Nothing?

CHAPTER 6 – ALL TOGETHER NOW

I think it's only fair I write a piece on my early influences, my mum Iris Lewis and my father Ernie. At Christmas my dad would get all his friends from the local boozer around on Christmas night. He would do his annual mimic of Al Jolson, with full face minstrel makeup, and suit and dickey bow.

He would do about three songs, 'Mammy' being his favourite. He was a true performer, and it must have been an attraction for my mum when they met at a dance hall in Warmley, Bristol one winter's night.

My mother had a fur coat, and at the end of the night noticing it was missing, looked out of the window to see Ernie waving it at her, saying, *"If you want it back, you must let me walk you home!"* How could she refuse!

My Nan Olive worked at Bristol Zoo for many years. She used to wear a fur hat with hat pins attached. Once, after her shift at the zoo she put her fur hat on for the journey home. *"OUCH"*, something had hurt her head as she put her hat on. 'Must have been my hat pin.' she thought. Later in the week she had a swelling right in the middle of her forehead. Confused she went to the doctor.

"I'm not sure what we are dealing with here." he told her, *"We will have to lance it to investigate."*

The doctor took his scalpel and cut it open, and to his amazement it was full of spiders! What had happened at the zoo is a banana spider had got into her hat and laid eggs in her head; this would leave the baby spiders to eat their way out when hatched and have a ready meal!

She was a funny old stick my Nan. She once had a small monkey who totally wrecked her house. She was very eccentric.

I'm sure, my father's upbringing was a hard one in Wales, and to earn money as a teenager he was a boxer in the fairgrounds and hunted rabbits in the Welsh mountains to sell. He had two brothers, Bill and Freddy. Freddy died young from meningitis. My dad blamed himself for his death because he used to spar box with him and being the better boxer he handed out more punishment than he received. When Freddy died my father refused to get out of bed for weeks.

In his younger days my father had jet black hair; he told me he dyed his hair with hedgehog oil. He would catch a hedgehog, wrap it in clay and cook it. When he unwrapped the clay from the animal the spines would fall off so not to get pricked.

The family moved from Machine Meadow in Pontypool, South Wales, also known as 'The Puzzle' to locals, to Bristol just before the Second World War. The house in Wales was a small terraced dwelling and was occupied by two families; one upstairs and one down stairs.

In the 50's and 60's my grandfather ran illegal gambling in the back room of his house in Alsop Road in Kingswood, Bristol. My mother Iris would serve drinks for the punters and keep a watchful eye at the front door.

Although I never met him, my father's dad could only be described as a small stocky and sometimes violent man. From the stories my mother had told me in the past, his wife terrified my older sisters.

The trend carried on in later years as my father Ernie took bets for horse racing in the local public houses.

He also distributed pools coupons. Pools coupons were very much the same as today's lottery, except it was based around football results. You had to pick eight teams each to draw in a match to win, and if you did the rewards were high. My sisters took it in turns to deliver and collect the coupons from regular customers each Friday night. When one sister got older the next younger one would take over, and so eventually it came down to me. I was paid 70 pence for a round of which I used my earnings to go to Eastville to watch Bristol Rovers every other Saturday. To escape school and go to football every other Saturday was bliss. I loved the excitement it brought.

In the 70's football violence was at its peak, and that was hardly surprising if all the secondary schools were handing out punishment on the same scale as we got at The Grange School for Boys. You had to get your frustrations out somewhere, and where better than on the terraces.

I used to catch the number 17 bus from Kingswood to Eastville. We always left early to catch the away supporters arriving at the ground. It was all running and chasing a lot of the time, maybe throwing a few bricks and bottles along the way.

One Saturday drinking in the pub at Eastville I remember a fight kicked off in the bar. Now I'm no fool, and being underage I made my escape via the front door. As I ran past the window a chair came smashing through it, just clearing my head. My mate Rob was still in the bar scrapping his way out. He eventually got out and we legged it to the football ground, laughing as we ran like hell.

Now it wasn't too long into the match when I noticed the back of Rob's coat was soaking wet. I knew this because in the infamous Tote End at the stadium, we had a chant that went like this, *"MOVE ALL TOGETHER.....MOVE ALL TOGETHER...."*

Everybody pushed forward at the same time, taking into account there was no seating in football grounds in those days, so I'm squashed up against Rob and I felt he was wet.

"Have you pissed yourself Rob?" I shouted at him. He replied, *"No. Why?"*

"You're fucking soaking wet!" I told him.

Rob turned, put his hand around the back of his coat and realised he was bleeding. He had been stabbed in the backside in the ruck at the pub and not even realised it!

That was the sort of adrenalin you would get at a football match. If my parents would have known they would have stopped me going.

I had two lucky escapes at Eastville; one was with the ICC West Ham United Intercity Crew, and one with The Chelsea Headhunters. Both very scary moments, they were men against boys sort of situations.

When Bristol Rovers drew Chelsea in the FA Cup at Eastville Stadium, is a time I will never forget. I arrived at the ground early, having walked there from home. It was an evening match and I couldn't wait to see some of the Chelsea players on the pitch. As usual I made my way to the turnstiles and I was in the ground by 6.45pm.

When you went to football matches on a regular basis, you recognised familiar faces, and you tended to stand in the same place. Taking into account there were no seats in the Tote End; it was standing only, so you could wander about and find the best view. The hardcore fans always went to the middle, and the not so tough ones to the sides, which is where I liked to stand.

The Tote End was quite full and kick off wasn't until 7.30pm and as I was looking around but couldn't see many familiar faces in the middle? I began to notice that not many of the crowd were wearing Rovers' scarves, which was unusual. Then from the middle of the Tote End came the chants, *"Chelsea! Chelsea!"* All the hardcore Rovers' fans had not arrived yet so it left the more mediocre soldiers in there with the Chelsea Headhunters! My first thoughts were, *"I gotta get out of here, fast; I'm in a whole world of shit!"* The last thing I wanted was a good kickin by the Chelsea fans. Once you were in the ground you couldn't get back out through the turnstiles so my only option was to get on the pitch, and I wasn't alone there.

Half the Rovers fans spilled onto the pitch, it was chaos, and the police came in heavy handed, swinging their batons and hitting anyone who got in the way; Rovers and Chelsea fans alike. Eventually the Chelsea fans were escorted out of the Tote End and we climbed back into the stand. It was an embarrassing moment for the Rovers' fans, the Tote End had been taken, it was the only time I can remember that ever happening, and the chants of, *"We took the Tote End,"* from the Chelsea fans didn't help either. And to top it all off, we lost the match!

Another match against West Ham United nearly ended up with the Tote End being taken on a sunny Saturday afternoon. At the time West Ham were my second favourite team, in fact they still are. I started to like them years previous when they had players like Bobby Moore, Trevor Brooking, Frank Lampard and Billy Bonds, to name a few. These guys were my heroes; I remember watching the 1970 World Cup, and the awesome Bobby Moore as Captain.

So with so much excitement bursting in me, me and a good mate of mine Shaun Taylor, set off early buzzing with the thought of seeing the Hammers. We arrived at the ground and made our way to the Tote End, which wasn't yet open. Outside the turnstiles it was packed, and me and Shaun were walking up to the turnstiles singing, *"We are the Tote End Boot Boys,"* totally unaware that we were in fact in the middle of all the West Ham supporters, also waiting to get into the Tote End.

As I said earlier we were just kids, and all these guys looked way older than us. Some were dressed smartly with long coats on and winkle picker shoes, shirts and ties, and some looked like they just came from working on the docks. A great big black guy grabbed me by the shoulder and bent down to my ear and in a Cockney accent said to me, *"You better fuck off mate!"* Me and Shaun ran like hell and got a few kicks up the arse as we were running, we didn't look back, we just ran! God knows how we got out alive!

At the matches, the police's best defence was the coppers on horses. You didn't stand a chance against them, and if you got too close to them you would get hit with the truncheon; it was a thugs' worst nightmare.

The stadium was very much like the shape of the old Wembley National stadium. It had a dog racing track around the pitch in which my father Ernie would race his greyhounds. One end of the goal mouths was the away supporters end and the other end, The Tote End. Sometimes the away supporters would run up on the railway track that ran alongside the Tote End and launch a stone throwing attack.

The best way to get a trophy was to get an away supporters' scarf, *"Give us that scarf kid or you're going home in an ambulance!"*

Small pockets of gangs from around Bristol would unite on Saturday afternoons. The whole thing was kind of tribal. It was a sad day when Eastville Stadium was finally demolished, it held great memories for me, from football, greyhound racing and speedway which took place every other Friday night.

It's not there anymore; they stuck an IKEA on it. My brother in-law, Dave who was a crane driver at the time, helped demolish the stadium and took one of the flood lights home for the memory. He still has that flood light to this day!

CHAPTER 7 – A CHANCE MEETING

My mother's brother, Ted, had a rough time under Lord Montgomery in the Second World War, in Egypt and didn't really like to talk about the war. I guess he saw a lot of bad things. He would get emotional if you asked him about it, and say, *"That's all over with now"*. I could see my mum cringe when I asked him about the war. He was such a soft looking bloke, with a short trimmed moustache, but nobody ever crossed him.

He enlisted in the Army after the Bristol airplane factory in Filton, Bristol where he worked was bombed.

At 11.59am on 25th September 1940 the first bomb of some three hundred or more was dropped on Filton by the Luftwaffe, killing more than ninety employees. He lost all his mates in the raid. One old guy took hold of him during the raid as he made his way to the air raid shelter, *"Don't go there my boy, come with me,"* and he led him to a field as the bombs began to drop. The shelter his mates were in took a direct hit and all but one died. The old man had saved his life.

Full of hate he soon found himself on the frontline in Egypt. For a man who was not well travelled it must have come as a shock to be in the dessert heat. To quench their thirst in the desert the soldiers would dig up pebbles and suck on them.

He later contracted malaria and was sent home to recover. When he became well again he was drafted to Belgium for service. It was in Belgium that there was a chance meeting between him and my father. They were amazed at the odds of them being in the same place at the same time, but unfortunately this did not have a happy ending.

One night they waited for the sun to go down and planned to sneak out of the army camp barracks and go to town for a night of drinking and then slip back in unnoticed.

Now the camp was some way off, so walking along the road they spotted an ambulance heading their way. Armed, they stood in the road and forced the Red Cross ambulance to stop and the driver to exit it. They drove off leaving the driver at the side of the road.

A mile or so later they realised the ambulance was carrying an injured German infantry soldier who was badly wounded. Maybe it was understandable at the time, but they later dumped the ambulance leaving the German soldier to die. Arriving late back at the camp, military police were waiting after the ambulance driver had made the alarm to the camp earlier. My father Ernie was arrested and did time in a military prison for his crimes.

He said it was the worst time of his life; a military prison was a lot worse than your average lockup. He had a small pan to use as a toilet, and some mornings the guards would come in and throw its contents over him. *"This place is a pigsty Lewis! Look what you've done; you've shit all over yourself. Clear it up you filthy bastard!"* This was followed by a good old fashioned kick in.

Around the same time my mother had a great escape after going to the local cinema in the Kingswood Bowling club building, which is now a shopping centre. She left just in time before a bomb dropped right where she was sitting. She recalled that everything from the shops was in the road, from men's suits to fish and of course you couldn't touch any of it. Looting laws were very strict; but it must have been tempting especially having to put up with rations. Had she stayed there two minutes longer I would not be here today.

My mother and my Nan would prefer to hide under the stairs than take the air raid shelter, and she had another lucky escape there! Unknown to them that they had a gas leak under the stairs, a neighbour would come to see if they were okay on her way back from the shelter, often finding them asleep. It wasn't until a gas check by the authorities that this came to light.

My mother used to play the piano, as did a lot of people back then, as TV was not about. She also encouraged my brother John to play music, buying him a guitar and a snare drum which was metallic blue as I remember it, but he never really took to it. He was more interested in motorbikes and cars. I think there's a few stolen motorbikes still buried in our old garden. My brother always had scrap cars at the top of the garden as well. When he wasn't about I would sit in them and pretend I was driving. I could never forget the smell of oil and leather those old cars had, and the sprung seats.

But he did love his music, and in the early 70's he had a great range of records that I used to play when he was out. I am still influenced by the music he had, from glam to Rock & Roll n roll. It was my brother who gave me my first decent stereo; it was the best I'd heard and would take some beating to this day.

In general my home life was a happy one. I was the youngest of seven, with five sisters and one brother, although it could have been eight had my mother not lost a boy at birth, and he would have been called David.

CHAPTER 8 – PUNK & DISORDERLY

It was 12.30am 1977, dark but humid and it had been a hot day. Along with my life time mate Tony Massey and his brother Paul, we were looking up at the biggest Union Jack we had ever seen, draped down the entire front of a two story flat on a housing estate. We were intent on nicking it and writing BRFC (Bristol Rovers Football Club) across the front. We would be the heroes of the then infamous Tote End at the Bristol Rovers football stadium in Eastville Bristol.

I don't know how but we got the flag down without anyone seeing. It weighed a bloody ton, and we ran like hell with this massive Union Jack; laughing all the way home, mission complete!

Now it didn't dawn on us that someone might be pissed off, waking up to find their Union Jack had gone on the day of the Queen's Silver Jubilee, the centre piece of their street party!

When I dragged myself out of bed I found my mum hovering over the radio in the kitchen, sleeves rolled up and apron on, shaking her head;

"What's the world coming to?" she said, *"Someone has nicked a Union Jack from the housing estate and police are investigating as it's worth a fortune. Bloody kids of today!"*

If only she had known it was under my bed. I suddenly didn't want it anymore; I was more scared of my mum finding out than the law catching up with us! We made a quick sale to a mate of ours and spent the rest of Jubilee day shitting ourselves! We wandered about various street parties feeling very unwanted; like lepers.

I remember having no knowledge of the punk movement that was going on in London at the time. My first taste of live music was a Rock & Roll band called Mud. Jeremy Bowden's brother Geoff was a few years older than me, and he had a spare ticket to see the band at the Locarno in the centre of Bristol, so I went along.

Geoff was a funny chap; he was bright and went to college. I remember him coming out with a school blazer on, rolled up at the sleeves and safety pins all over it. I said to him, *"What the hell are you wearing?"* He replied, *"Punk Rock in it!"*

So in the late 70's, early 80's, the ripples from the punk explosion in London finally hit the towns beyond the capital city, and so began a love affair that has lasted a life time.

After leaving school there were not many options in the way of work, so myself and friend Dave Pepworth took to stealing records from the local music store and selling them to a record collector we knew. It was at Dave's house that I first came into contact with a real set of drums, owned by his brother Danny.

Danny was a slim guy and super cool and man could he play drums. He was right up to date on the music scene and introduced me to The Tubes, an American band that were hitting the headlines in the music press for their on stage antics. It's only fair to say Danny was a big influence on me musically.

To be in a punk band was not just cool, but accessible to everyone, never before had so many bands formed at one time, some good, some bad, and some plain ugly. You didn't have to be musically trained or anything, it was all about making some noise. It was also about the clothes you wore; how I saw it buying clothes from a fashion shop was a no go, instead we bought our clothes from charity shops, especially shoes. In the charity shops you could find winkle pickers and one of my favorites was old ladies boots, they had fur inside them and a zip up the front, and the old men's coats were a favorite as well.

But it didn't take long for the fashion world to catch onto it, and before you could wink there were punk shops popping up everywhere selling bondage trousers and t-shirts and creepers.

When you look at punk in Bristol, the first name that springs to mind is The Vice Squad. I remember first seeing them at a church hall in Kingswood, playing with two other bands; The Piss Heads, and The Under Fives, which both were good bands.

The Vice Squad had it all, the image was great; Mark Hamblin on bass, tall with spiky hair; Dave Bateman on guitar, chewing gum; Shane Baldwin on drums, wearing the famous Motorhead t-shirt that he always did; and Becky Bondage on vocals, looking a million dollars. This gig was my first taste of real punk rock and remains one of the best gigs I've been to, despite the fighting that took place after the gig, but that was something I saw coming. I had my training at Eastville, Bristol Rovers football ground. With football violence at its peak you kind of had a sixth sense when something was going to kick off and you got out of the way. Not that the fighting was that bad after the gig, just a few bloody noses.

The Vice Squad went from strength to strength under the watchful eye of Simon Edwards, Bristol's punk guru. I don't think The Vice Squad got enough respect in Bristol. I mean this band were selling loads of records and entering the charts. Maybe not kid friendly enough for some, but they were pioneers in Bristol and surrounding areas in the punk movement.

When Becky left, Shane and Dave formed Sweet Revenge along with Jon Chilcott on bass and vocals; Lucy and Di from Balloon Music on backing vocals, and after the first record came out; Andy Rope on lead vocals, and at different times, Rich Lacey and Tim Galley on guitars.

I first saw them at The Granary in Bristol and they were great. The Granary was always a top music venue in Bristol, although the music genre as a whole was not my scene. I did see The Vice Squad there and The Stranglers, but it was usually progressive rock bands, and to be honest as a punk rocker you didn't get the best reception from the army of Hells Angels that frequented the place, in fact it was bloody scary!

The first time I went there I walked in just looking at the floor so not to piss anyone off, and as I was walking up the stairs there was some biker beating the hell out of some kid on the stairs who was obviously, right out of the game on some type of mind bending drug. When the biker had finished kicking him, the guy looked up and said, *"Peace man!"* Even the biker looked shocked, and wandered off into the dark.

It was a great venue though, despite the lack of punk bands, and a shame it closed its doors to become flats and a fish restaurant!

Competition was pretty fierce among bands in Bristol at the time. Bands like The Glaxo Babies, The Spics, and

Essential Bop were packing the crowds in. Although Bristol artistes found themselves swimming against the tide, as record companies seemed to prefer acts from London and Manchester and at the time a DJ was someone who played records before and after the real thing.

The only other band from Bristol to break the mould was the 1977 punksters The Cortina's, named after the car, Ford Cortina because it was crap. The band split in 1978, and guitarist Nick Sheppard went on to join The Clash after the sacking of Mick Jones and recorded the album 'Cut The Crap'.

'This is England' reached the charts at number 24. Sheppard was quoted saying, *"I remember sitting in a different city watching it, thinking this isn't a band."*

The Clash split shortly afterwards.

The punk movement was more than just a fashion to me; it was a way of expressing that we have all had enough. It was the best thing to happen since the birth of The Beatles in the 60's.

As a youth I enjoyed horror books and movies, the similarity between punk and Mary Shelley's book, Frankenstein are so very similar. Man creates monster, and then when he sees what an abomination he has created, he rejects it, it repulses him. The monster is an outcast, but he is misunderstood. Much the same as punk, society makes the monster, and then rejects it.

The first band I was in was called The Assassinators, influenced by The Clash's first album bought for me on a Christmas by my sister Janet. I'd never heard anything like it before, and purchased The Damned's first album 'Damned Damned Damned'. I'd heard The Damned album at the local youth club at the bottom of New Cheltenham Road. It was called The Made Forever Youth Club and our youth leader was a Welshman called Neil Hunt. He was a cool guy and down on the streets with the kids. He would ask us what records to buy for the club, so we had access to all the new punk bands.

The club itself was built with corrugated tin on the outside and a prefab building attached at the side, it wasn't the best of construction but it was a good place to hang out as a teen.

With my first weeks wages of £17.00 I bought 'Generation X' album.

Now I don't want to harp on about how little money we had, but for an example when we went to a chip shop we would get one bag of chips between six of us and ask for the scrumps. This was the batter that fell off the fish and sausages. Can you imagine health and safety getting hold of that now? And although we should have been fat you could have found more meat on a sparrow's leg! That was it from there on, punk rock ruled!

What with Thatcherism, miners' strikes, and generally no money in my pockets, or anyone else's, for that matter, myself, Rob Ryall, Shaun Smallman, and Terry Cook set about forming The Assassinators. Shaun really looked the part, he was one of those kids who had great jet black spiky hair, he wore a long old man's coat, as did we all, and had a dead bird pinned to it and a used condom! This always got some looks when we went into town to Virgin Records in the centre of Bristol to hang out. And that was exactly what we wanted; we wanted people to notice us.

Terry had a good job, and was the only one who had any money. He bought a peavey amp and Stratocaster copy. Terry was a lovely geezer but suffered a stroke of bad luck when he got into a fight over money and suffered some brain damage. Rob borrowed some cash from his dad and bought a bass and amp, as I remember, and I got a loan from a loan company that I never paid back to this day, and bought a drum kit.

We walked into the drum store and told the geezer, *"We got one hundred and fifty pounds, sort us out."* Lesson number one, don't tell the guy how much money you got, he saw us coming and we walked out with an assortment of bits and pieces from about twenty different kits! Shaun got a microphone and amp from somewhere, and so, the birth of The Assassinators.

We never really did a lot; in fact I don't think we ever played a gig! Although we did have a chance to play with The Vice squad, and we shit ourselves. As I remember it I saw Mark Hamblin (Vice Squad bassist) about a week before the gig and he informed me it had been cancelled - thank god!

We were popular with some girls though, who used to come and watch us practice from time to time, and that seemed enough, but we never really took it seriously.

Rob used to mix tracks on an old cassette player of all our favorite punk songs, recording all the best bits and mixing them into one track. A few years later the charts were bombarded with the same thing but with disco music; they called it Stars on 45, and the idea must have come off the street. If only we would have been a bit more sharp at the time eh!

We all kind of drifted apart after a year, but I was still fascinated by the music of that time, and did not intend on giving up just yet.

So came the second band, The Rout. Myself on guitar, Mark Austin [Austin] on drums, and Danny Hooper on bass.

I met Austin at the bottom of my street one night when I was just sat there listening to some recordings we had done with the Assassinators on an old mono cassette player. He couldn't believe it was us playing on it, and so began a friendship that has lasted to the present day.

Austin had a place at his parents' that we could play around in, and I left the drums set up there so he could use them when he liked. He took to it like a fish to water and became the drummer.

By this time I had bought a Satellite Gibson copy, it was a great guitar that was distorted as soon as you plugged it in, but I did get fed up with it, and decided it had to go, so I smashed it into a wall, and the bloody wall broke! It was indestructible; I think we ended up burning it like some sort of sacrifice at the end of my garden.

My mother (or Ice as we called her) was a great help with anything musical I did over the years, in fact she helped me buy my first genuine Gibson guitar. A Gibson SG. She was immensely proud of me playing guitar and was always encouraging me. However, I don't think Ice liked punk rock; she would prefer music from the musicals.

Danny had a massive Hiwatt cab and played a Fender bass. He also bought a Rickenbacker, but didn't like it, so he went back to the Fender.

Our first gig came out of the blue, when Nigel Rocket, who went on to form Onslaught, came to our practice and asked if we would play at the local youth club, named the Summit. I said yes we will do it! I remember after he had gone Austin and Dan saying, *"What the fuck did you say yes for?"*

Well I got my own way and we played the gig with Shaun Smallman helping with the vocals. I think it was okay for our first gig, but the drums got wrecked, Keith Moon style.

As far as success goes, we had a good time with the early Rout as a three piece, playing youth clubs, back rooms in pubs etc., and as the greatest moment as a three piece, we played with The UK Subs at The Tropic Club in St Paul's Bristol, and I still have the desk recording.

One thing I remember about meeting Charlie Harper, the lead vocalist, was Dan introducing himself and saying, *"What the fuck you drinking orange juice for?"*

Dan had a way with words, a 'what you see is what you get' kind of guy. He was very unpredictable and played the Rock & Roll lifestyle how it should be.

By this time we had been to our first studio, a place called The Fox Hole, out in the sticks, where we recorded three tracks; two of our own, and one Sex Pistols cover 'Submission', taken from the 'Never Mind The Bollocks' album.

The first of our efforts was called 'Cold Streets', and was all about seeing the industrial workforce going to work in the morning, along with their sandwich boxes and hobnail boots. That was a time when everyone seemed to work in a factory, as I mentioned earlier, and it was something I could relate too.

The second track, *'Noise a Bolo'* was a more up-tempo track and in my view, the best of the three.

We fell out with the studio owner, whose name was Martin something. He said he was going to do this and that, but it never happened, and that was the end of that studio for us. Not the end of The Rout though, we decided we could do with another member, and found it in a guy called Aid Goth, who was in a band called 'Smiles' with his brother Kevin.

They had a few good tracks. One that sticks in my mind was called 'Anything Will Do to Hide Reality'. The title speaks for itself. Aid had a great image, he was real gothic style, long hair and all, and an all round good guy. His bedroom was painted black, had loads of mirrors everywhere, and he liked to keep rats as pets. While Aid was in the band we made more recordings at Diamond Studios with an engineer called Pete Diamond who was a real old hippy. I remember seeing him playing a part in a TV series called Casualty on the BBC. He played a thug, and we all ribbed him about it for ages.

"Yeah, knock out." was one of his favorite sayings, but god knows what he thought of us.

With four songs recorded I sent a few off for a compilation album a band was putting together in Southampton. They were called Red Letter Day, and were a Clash orientated band. I liked them a lot. We went to play with them in Southampton at this place by the docks, along with one other band, and as I remember it, it was a great night.

We did get on the compilation with a track called 'I Know More Than You'. We had a great response from this one with a small fan base in the USA, and we were getting regular mail from fans overseas. We also did a few interviews with some fanzines, which was fun.

It was a long and drawn out process to get any kind of communication done at that time. With computers not available, it was postage stamp after postage stamp, and to use the phone at home was out of the question unless you fancied a thump from your old man.

I recently bumped into an old Rout fan that still had the compilation, and told me The Manic Street Preachers were on it as well, which did give me a bit of a surprise.

Looking back it could have been them who played with us at the docks in Southampton, but I can't say for sure.

We had some good success with Aid in the band, and played to a good following at the Beerkieller in Bristol one rainy Sunday night; this was the height of the Rout with Aid.
There was one time when we had a gig come up with The UK Subs, but Aid was in Australia at the time. Dan and Paul Riddle were outside touting tickets and a crew turned up demanding free entry as they had come to see their best mate Aid.
"Well that's fucking strange." said Riddle, "He aint even in the country." and sent them packing.

So we went back to a three piece for this one and it was a great show with Dan right on form. One magazine said the bass player looked like he was chewing on a mouthful of wasps! I've still got the recording from that gig, and it's still great to listen to.

We had our first release on vinyl in the mid 80's, on a compilation album called 'Underground Resistance.' We recorded the track 'Time' at an old manor house in Yorkshire; this was our first taste of a real good studio and engineer. I don't recall the engineer's name, but he worked with Bob Marley a bit, and told us some stories of Mr Marley always carrying a carrier bag of grass with him everywhere. God knows what he made of us? We recorded and mixed the track in a single day. Apparently it sold well in Sweden, but we never saw a penny for all our efforts.

As we began to get more success, Dan began to drink more. I remember one night at a place called The Railway, a huge following came along. Dan was so wrecked he fell off the stage, Austin threw his drum sticks out in the crowd, and a mass scrap started.

The venue shut not long after that, although we did not feel responsible for the big scrap, as at the time the owner couldn't handle the big crowd and stopped serving beer. Big mistake; he had one angry crowd on his hands.

At the time I always preferred people smoking dope than drinking beer, of all the things to legalise; they pick the stuff that turns you into an arsehole were my thoughts.

Another funny thing happened when we played The Bristol Council Club; we had been using pyrotechnics at some gigs with no problems. As we ripped into a song called 'Unknown Origin', the pyrotechnics should have gone off via a foot switch, but didn't! Dan went to investigate, and as he was about two feet away, 'BANG' they went off! He played the rest of the set with no eyebrows! We all pissed ourselves laughing and a few of the crowd who hung around afterwards asked how we planned it!

We carried on recording at Sam's Studio in St Paul's were we met Shane Baldwin from the Vice Squad, and Sooty the engineer, who was working on Chaotic Discord recordings.

Austin and I did backing tracks for the album 'Very Fucking Bad', which was a great bit of fun after getting pissed in the local boozer before we recorded. The album was taking the piss out of Michael Jackson's album 'Bad'.

Dan was a great bass player and when he left the band we missed him dearly. He has not played since which is a shame.

We got a new bass player, who was already a friend; his name was Andy Smith (Smitty).

A year had passed since Dan left and we took up practice residence in the shape of Austin's back room in Cecil Road, Kingswood. The room was full of hash smoke within ten minutes of every practice, and at times I could not make out Austin on the drums because of the smoke. I have fond memories of this time.

We started doing a few covers and stuck with the name The Rout; although it was a different direction. We found ourselves playing Blockheads tracks, and Joe Jackson etc. We did get gigs a bit easier playing covers, but always stuck a few of our own in for good measure.

We did a recording at a place in Bath called Kosan. It was a great studio, and the likes of Tears for Fears, and The Stranglers used it for rehearsals etc. I remember the engineer telling us of how Jet Black of The Stranglers used to stay up all night programming drum samples after a hard day at the studio.

We recorded a track called 'The Separate', and had Carol Ryall doing backing for us. She was a great singer and we got to know her through Rob Ryall from The Assassinators.

At the same time me and Austin decided to give music promoting a try at The Snooker Club in Kingswood.

One great time that sticks in my mind was when we were invited to a party at Kosan, which we went along to. It was full of stuffy student type people and I thought, *"This is shit. Shall we go?"*

Then in walked Hugh Cornwell, of The Stranglers who just happened to be my hero at the time. We stayed and had a good chat with him, and left at the same time. Since then I've met Hugh a few times and found him to be a true gentleman.

Promoting was going good at The Snooker Club, and we put on bands like, The UK Subs, Chelsea, The Vibrators, and some good local acts.

We also got involved with a thing called National Music Day which was set up by Roger Daltrey and a few others. We held an all day event at The Horseshoe pub, on Siston Common and Radio 2 were there to cover the day.

The Horseshoe was a funny pub; it was punks, bikers, and the gun club, all with their own tables in designated parts of the pub. It was friendly and nobody bothered anyone else. The Rout played a track on air called 'Through the Window', and we were also interviewed by the station; but I said very little, because I couldn't stand the sound of my own voice; I sound like a farmer!

We also met a guy called Dave Brayley, who used to hire us a P.A. He became a good mate and went on to be a successful Bristol promoter, first working The Mauritania in Park Street, and then The Fleece & Firkin.

We watched The Meteors at The Mauritania as one of Dave's guests. This is one gig I won't forget as there was one hell of a fight! I recall talking to Dave Ayres, who had a tattoo shop in Old Market, Bristol called 'Skin Deep'.

Just before the band went on Dave took his shirt off in anticipation, and as soon as the band started he dived up front and so the scrap began!

Very sadly Dave was killed in a motorcycle accident in 2009 and will always be remembered for his fabulous tattooing.

Our next addition to the band was a keyboard player called Duncan; he was one of those guys that could do anything, play drums, guitar, and sing. He was very talented. Duncan went on to be a teacher in London, so didn't stay long, but the time he was with us was great.

From the time after Duncan left, we kind of lost our way with what direction we should go in. Punk was generally forgotten about by then, and we wandered aimlessly from cover track to cover track. We finally split, and so the end of The Rout.

With a lot of time to think about things, me and Austin decided life just aint the same without a band, so we approached Bob Watson who was playing around with a few friends of ours at the time. Bob had nothing to prove, he was a former member of a band called Misdemeanor, who had the same manager as U2, and having played with U2, and also The Boomtown Rats as support. Bob knew what it was all about. Misdemeanor had been on TV, played the Moulin Rouge in Paris, had a great fan base, and why the hell they split up I will never know!

Bob has told us some great stories about Misdemeanor. One that springs to mind is when they played at Weston Super Mare with Gene October and Chelsea. Their sound engineer on that occasion was somewhat of an idiot as I understand it. With the band into their set, the drummer of Misdemeanor was so unhappy with the sound that he jumped over the drums and chased the poor guy right out of the venue, and he never returned to finish the sound for Chelsea!

And the time when after playing with U2 at an after gig party, Bob's girlfriend got pissed off with him and pushed him in the swimming pool, only to be followed by Bono, and just about everyone else there, leaving egg on his girlfriends face, as Bob tells it.

Just one more of Bob's stories with Misdemeanor, one that still makes me laugh when I think of it. Bob was playing a gig in Crickhowell in Wales, which is a small village in the Welsh valleys. At the time he was young, free and single so he chatted up the landlady of the venue they were playing and she told Bob her relationship with her boyfriend had gone sour and they had split up. Bob saw his chance and was all over her like a cheap suit, and ended up in her bed.

Now Bob didn't know at the time but her boyfriend came into the venue while they were in bed. Learning that his ex girlfriend was in bed with Bob the ex boyfriend took an axe and rushed up stairs in a rage and began to smash the door down with the axe. Bob and the landlady sat bolt up in bed as the guy smashed through the door with the axe in hand. Before Bob could even try to make and escape the guy was in the room. He shouted, *"I want my fucking Def Leopard album!"*, and picked the album up from the corner of the room and left! I don't think Bob could ever get his head around that situation, he thought he was done for.

Anyway back to the master plan. So we had Austin, Bob Watson, and me, but no bass player. We were looking for someone a bit off the wall, and we found it in Jason Stallard, ex Onslaught member. All we needed now was a name.

We came up with some real humdingers, like 'Chrome Dome', 'The Bollock Brothers', etc. etc., It wasn't until one Thursday night at the local boozer called The Kings Arms, that we all got pissed, and as you do, discussed the music business in general, moaning and groaning about Kylie Minogue etc., when I said, *"It's all a load of bullshit Vic."* Austin piped up with, *"Fuck it, how about The Bolsheviks?"* We all fell about laughing, and that was it The Bolsheviks it was from then on.

No great political statement, no thought of genius, just drunk and pissed off with the music business; our plan was to exploit it to its full potential. The Bolsheviks were born.

We started rehearsals in the back room of The Kings Arms boozer, where we held our first gig. You could get about eighty people in there at a push; it was dark and dingy, perfect really.

We let people in for free that night and it was packed; a very good start.

We played often at The Wunderbar, in Midsomer Norton, near Bath, and we were asked to play the last Midsomer Norton Festival in August of that year. The problem was I was due to go on holiday the day before so had to cut my holiday short, which I didn't mind, and had support from my wife, Sally.

On the day it was sunny, and we had Sally and Austin's girlfriend, Marie, walk around in black fur coats, Russian hats, and boots, which raised a few eyebrows.

Before we went on, the stage was filled with dry ice, and as I picked up my guitar, I noticed Jason Stallard had found a fire extinguisher on entering the stage. He walked up to the microphone and shouted, *"FIRE!"* He then let off the fire extinguisher to the crowd's horror!

That was the thing with Jason, your never knew what he was going to do next, he is an extraordinary guy. The gig went great, and the Bath Chronicle Newspaper gave us a good write up, and found Jason's antics amusing.

Our next gig was at The Fleece & Firkin in Bristol and after the effect the two girls had, walking around intimidating people, we decided to try it again, this time we would have them on stage with us. It went down really well so we used it again and again. However, it didn't always go well. At one gig we played on a farm; it was a good set up, with us playing on a lorry trailer. There were ostriches running about, and the food and beer was in abundance. I don't think anyone there had seen us before, because when the girls got on stage they thought they were strippers! It nearly got out of hand, but luckily they got the joke and no harm was done.

There was another funny time when the girls were carrying plastic guns at a gig, and were asked to put them away as they were frightening people! That was bizarre but understandable.

Well we went on and on with this line up, but eventually Jason Stallard left the band. He was a good bass player and still remains a friend.

So come forth Lee Williams! Lee was young when he joined the band, and we put him straight in the deep end, as our next gig was with The Damned at the Beerkieller, in Bristol.

Captain Sensible watched our sound check and shouted, *"Fucking crap!"* at the end; we took that as a good omen.

We had a good gig with The Damned and found Captain Sensible a good laugh.

With Lee now firmly in the band, we began to write new songs with Lee's influence being important, and being the youngest, he had different views on music as the rest of the band. This was refreshing and seemed to work out.

So we began on The Bolsheviks' first album, *'Wot U Lookin at'* We found a studio in Kewstoke, Weston Super Mare; it was small, but the guy seemed to know what he was doing so we went with it because it was cheaper than what we had looked at in Bristol and Bath.

The guys name was Martin Nicholls and as it goes he is the best engineer we have had to date; although he really does work you hard to get the results.

In the past at other studios we have been in they just let us get on with it. So at first it came as a bit of shock, being told it wasn't good enough, and to try harder this time.

Austin did struggle with Martin at the beginning, but now they are good buddies. Austin does not like being told what to do, it's part of his personality that makes him what he is. He will call a spade a spade, something I've always admired about him.

We recorded three tracks over a two day period, putting the drums, bass, and guitars down on day one, and mixing on day too.

We recorded 'Blame', 'Comrades Confused', and 'Love in Vain', which was a Ruts cover about heroin abuse. We felt strongly about this song as it was written by Malcolm Owen of The Ruts, who later died of a heroin overdose. It's one of those songs that a drug abuser would understand, but has a different meaning to someone that doesn't use drugs.

Bob put some great Reggie tones down, and we didn't mess a lot with it in the mix, we just kept it a bit raw.

The next track was 'Blame', one Bob had written and still remains a favourite. We over dubbed the guitars and Bob over dubbed the vocals. For me it's one of those recordings when you actually get it right.

The third track 'Comrades Confused', we struggled with. The music was fine, but we had not prepared properly for the vocals as it was a new song. Bob ended up doing most of the vocals. Since then we will not record a track unless we have gigged it and played it for ages, because there's nothing worse than thinking, *"Shit, wish I would have done this or that different."* We ended up using 'Comrades Confused' for a bonus track on the album.

We also put in a few Russian tracks for fillers in-between songs, 'Kalinka', and 'Cossack Patrol.' Overall we were pleased with two of the three tracks.

With no financial backing, we gigged hard for a year before we got back into the studio; we needed money for not only the studio, but also pressing the CD and covers. Our next visit we would finish the album.

`We recorded 'Animal Lover', 'Pantyphobia', 'Radio', and 'Kremlin'.

I penned and sang 'Animal Lover'. It's a song about beastiality, with a double meaning, and you can take it either way. We used this track to open the album.

The second is 'Pantyphobia'. I also wrote and sang this one; it's about the coming of the thong, the newly found women's underwear of the time, pretty self explanatory. It's not a track intended to be taken seriously.

'Radio' is one of Bob's and reminds me of teenage adolescents. He sang this one, and we always played it at the end of our set. It's a very strong number, and we were pleased how this one came out.

'Kremlin' was written and sang by Bob. It's a real James Bond style track, 'From Russia with Love' sort of thing, and for me, one of the best tracks on the album.

As with all the tracks we have, input from each member was a must. It's how we worked. Every song has a little bit of each member in it.

With all the recording done, and the art work completed by Sally, we had a CD that was ours and nobody owned any part of it, apart from the band.

We had some good reviews. Gary Bushell liked it which opened up a new door for another project. Mr Bushell not only writes for the tabloid, but also plays in an Oi band called 'The Gonads'; Gary is considered the Godfather of Oi in the UK.

Anyway the guitar player for The Gonads at the time, who lives in New York, heard Blame on the website and contacted us to do a track for a tribute album for 'The Four Skins'. We were going to record it at The Whitehouse studios, but it was Christmas time, and Martin told us he doesn't work at Christmas. So we found a small studio in Bath which was cheap and we recorded it there. It was a digital recording and it was bloody freezing there. Austin had been on the beer the night before, and for some reason I used a Marshall amp they had at the studio and not my own. The results were a little disappointing, but we got away with it, playing a track for the tribute album called, 'Justice'.

The CD took nearly a year to get sorted out, but when it finally arrived we were pleased with the way it looked, and the distribution was in Europe and the USA, but we did feel we could have done better with the recording. But hey, that's something you have to put up with when you are on a shoestring budget.

By the time the album came out we had recruited Paul, the singer from a band called 'Lux'. Paul is an extraordinary guy; he is six foot tall, Afro Caribbean with long dreadlocks, leather jeans and just looks like a rock star; he has a real aura about him.

In Stinky Turners' (lead singer with 'The Cockney Rejects') autobiography, co-written by Gary Bushell, there's an issue on fascism in Oi music and a reference to The Bolsheviks who played on a Four Skins' tribute album; Stinky turner asked the question, *"Does it sound like fascism to you?"*

One of the great bands I admired for years was 'Lux', when Paul was singing for them. Strongly influenced by 'The Cramps', they were great to watch live. Some years after most of the original members had left; I went to watch them in a pub in Bristol city centre.

I'd always been friendly with front man Lux (Paul) and asked him after the gig if he would like to come and jam with us. He seemed interested and came along to our next rehearsal.

Some of the band, apart from Lee, were unsure about this, but I persuaded them and after our first get together we all decided he just had to be in The Bolsheviks.

`Paul is a unique character; to look at him you would expect to find him back stage drinking a bottle of vodka, but in fact more often you would find him with a cup of tea. He is like an eccentric English gentleman in his manor.

The timing was good when Paul joined as we were about to work on our second album 'Nuclear Dogs'. Again we used Whitehouse Studios for this album, and the first track we had written with Paul was 'C U Later'; which was to be the first track on the album. The opening sequence was in mono for the first few seconds to give it impact when the stereo hit in, and it worked a treat. For some, this is our best album.

In 2004 I went back to promoting with my wife Sally and Mike Hutson, a good friend of ours and a real gentleman. We started to promote at The Rotunda Club in Kingswood, Bristol, and on our first night we put on 'The Beat', a Ska band from the 80's. This gig sold out and we thought we were on to a good thing. Working with Ranking Roger from 'The Beat' was a no hassle affair; he and the entire band were very easy going but very professional.

We also put on 'The Anti Nowhere League', at an all day event, 'Splodge Nessabounds', and a very slim Buster Blood Vessel with 'Bad Manners', 'The UK Subs', 'Sham 69', 'The Selector', 'Peter & The Test Tube Babies', 'GBH', and loads of other bands.

We felt we were doing the community well by putting on acts like these, but found it hard to compete with inner city venues and lack of input from the venue owners; so in 2006 we called it a day.

The funny thing was that most of the support came from outside of Kingswood, which did confuse me some?

It was at one of the Rotunda gigs that I met Keith who plays in 'Picture Frame Seduction' and was setting about making his own record label, 'Cult Jam Records'. So when I saw an advertisement asking for demos, I sent over a Bolsheviks' demo. He liked it and wanted us on board.

This was a big break for us as the distribution was really good, going worldwide! We already had the songs recorded so it was just a case of getting them mastered, and sending it off to be coated etc. And so, the birth of 'Nuclear Dogs'.

Sally designed the covers and did the art work, and in August 2006 it was released. There was one track that didn't make the album I'm sorry to say, it was a cover of a UK Subs track 'CID', but we called it 'KGB'.

I rang Charlie Harper, from the Subs and asked if we could record it, and he said not a problem, as it's unlikely it would make number one in the charts! Charlie is, in my mind, one of the most respected names in punk and deserves a Knighthood!

Our first gig to launch the album went pear shaped! It was at The Reckless Engineer in Temple Meads, Bristol. The PA blew up after twenty minutes. I was gutted. The guy who hired it to us never got any more business out of us and neither did he get paid.

The last time we played there, Fish from 'Marillion' turned up, but unfortunately we were without Paul as he was ill. After, we had a good old chat with Fish and he got us a few beers in. The following week he was on 'The Weakest Link', a quiz show on TV, and he bloody won it!

The CD's were not ready; the PA blew up after six songs. It was a disaster!

The next gig was at an all day event at the King Billy in Oldland Common, and disaster struck again when a stunt went wrong, and Paul ended up with two broken ribs! Someone in the crowd caught this disaster on film and funny enough it is now one of the top 50 clips on 'You've Been Framed'.

It seemed as if it was one step forward and two steps back, pissing in the wind, but I'm glad to say things went on the up after that.

There was one more incident that I will mention, and that's when we played TJ's in Newport. We took a fifty two seater coach to the gig full of fans, and to be fair it was a real good night. We were treated well by the promoter, and played okay. It was on the way back that it all kicked off. Football songs being chanted from the back of the coach and fifty one people with a belly full of beer, and I thought at the time, *"This aint good!"*

There was a commotion at the back of the coach as we entered Bristol, and all hell broke loose. It really was nasty stuff, with blood and broken noses; that sort of thing. The driver of the coach was terrified, and there was some damage to the coach as well, which we had to pay for; we never did get the bill.

We seemed to be dogged by bad luck; just when we nearly got there, something would always happen or get in the way.

The saddest day I had with the Bolsheviks was one rainy night playing The Fleece & Firkin in Bristol. Austin, my old mate Tony Massey and I had arranged to meet another good friend of ours at The Seven Stars Inn which is right next to The Venue we were playing.

We were meeting Dean, better known to his mates as Humpty. Humpty is the sort of guy you want to bump into anywhere you go, he is always smiling and likes a good time, he has that gangster look about him, always smartly dressed and smokes like a trooper, cigarette in hand and grinning like a Cheshire cat. He is one of the good guys you don't come across very often.

Apart from finding some guy having intercourse with some girl in my changing room, the gig went well, we played well, packed up and headed for a club in Kingswood called Barcelona for a few late drinks. It had been a brilliant night and we said goodbye to Humpty as he left for the kebab shop, still smiling and still smoking his cigarettes.

The next day I got a call from Tony saying Humpty's dead. He had gone home and tried to cook some chips and set the place on fire. In his panic to put out the fire he fell down the stairs of his flat and broke his neck.

I still think of him from time to time, he was such a great guy and I for one miss his presence.

In April 2007 we played at an event in Camber Sands, Sussex; a three day punk extravaganza! There were some great bands on the bill, Cockney Rejects, Anti Nowhere League, Splodge, Sham 69, Vice squad, Sponge, PFS, to name a few.

When we arrived, it looked like something from a 50's holiday camp; bloody awful. There were skinheads everywhere, and keeping in mind we had a black singer, it was a bit tense to say the least.

Paul (Lux) was no stranger to racist remarks, having grown up in a predominantly white area of Bristol.

As soon as we got to the bar to get a drink Paul just happened to pick a spot where there were three or four skinheads stood, all dressed in white Levi jeans, Doctor Martin boots, white shirts and red bracers and they had their eyes firmly fixed on Paul. Paul walked straight up to them and said, *"Have you seen my spear, I'm lost without it!"*

The skinheads fell about laughing and bought Paul a beer. He had a knack of how to deal with things in a situation; he was always one step in front.

Everything went off okay and we stayed up all night partying in our room with fellow rockers, Dogzuki, and True Sounds of The Revolution, but I couldn't help thinking, *"Is this where punk has ended up, a bloody Pontins holiday camp?"*

The following week an earthquake hit Kent, pity it didn't go as far as Camber Sands!

After the album 'Nuclear Dogs' had ran its course, we decided there was one last album left in the tank. We started recording at The Whitehouse studio again and wanted this next album to be more of our own; we wanted it to sound more current than the last one but still with punk leanings.

It has all the signatures to a Bolsheviks' album with some real heavy bass lines on some of the songs by Lee Williams. The songs ranged from lyrics about the conflict between the

East and the West, right down to the Aborigines in Australia. It was varied and some tracks sound like heavy metal and some like rockabilly. We were generally pleased with the outcome, and Bob mastered the album himself.

At this point I decided to form our own record label 'Red Square Records' and our new album that we now decided to call 'Action Reaction' was released. The album launch was to be held at The Polish Club in Clifton, Bristol, and with the usual promotion push we had a great audience.

Also on the bill were rockabilly outfit, 'Kill Van Helsing' and we had Burlesque dancers as well which were fabulous!

Everything went off swimmingly that night; it got messy in the changing room but it was just a great Rock & Roll affair. But, as in all bands, when you're with the same people for long periods of time, cracks begin to appear. We began bickering about petty things, and if a gig was booked it was hell trying to keep everyone happy.

There were times when we just couldn't be in the same room; it's very hard to explain what happens in a band when things go wrong, because you are all so close, it's like a family. Eventually Bob decided he had enough and quit the band, it was a sad day indeed.

I still wanted to carry on with The Bolsheviks and put our problems behind us, so we got another guitar player in the form of Dave Devonald, a true demon of the guitar. Dave is a great chap, I've a lot of time for him, he fitted in just perfect and we threw him in head first with a gig in Newcastle with The Vice Squad.

We tried to write more songs in between gigs but I think by then we had all lost our thirst for The Bolsheviks, and it eventually fizzled out. I don't regret a minute of my time in that band as I've so many good memories and the fun we all had.

Red Square Records kept me busy for a while. I released The Bolsheviks' album and a single and released two compilation albums by various artistes of which I named the album 'Jilted Generation Volume 1 and 2', a Sick Livers' album and a few other singles.

I enjoyed the Jilted Generation albums because I got to choose who went on them; selfish I know, but the end product was great if I should say so myself.

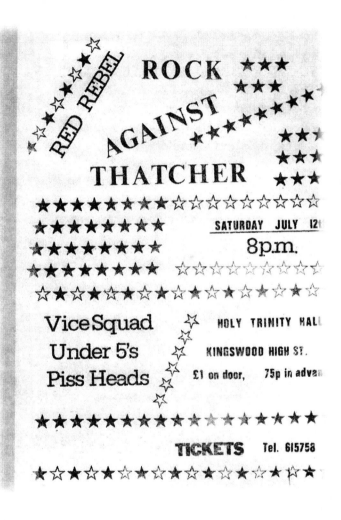

Original first gig poster

The early Bolsheviks, left to right; Louie Lewis, Bob Watson,
Mark Austin

Bolsheviks Album Launch

The Oi Godfather Gary Bushell

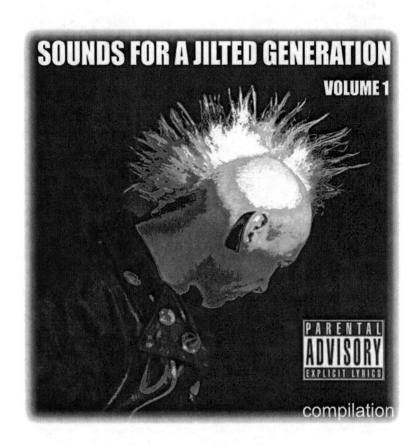

The first release for Redsquare Records

The Bolsheviks' 'Action Reaction' album launch @ The Polish Club

Back stage with Misdemeanor & Bananarama, left to right:
Phil Rice, Kevin McFadden, Sara Dallin, Bob Watson, Steve
Capaldi, Keren Woodward

Bristol Polyents presents

CORTINAS
EUROPEANS
THE MEDIA

ON SUNDAY 24 TH SEPTEMBER

AT

BRISTOL
LOCARNO

Tickets : £ 1.25 in advance

£ 1.50 on door

The Cortinas @ Bristol Lacarno

Punks outside Virgin Records during a Vice Squad
photoshoot, 1982

The Vice Squad, left to right; Dave Bateman, Shane Baldwin,
Beki Bondage, Mark Hamblin

The Rotunda Club, Kingswood, Bristol

The Kings Arms, Kingswood, left to right; Danny the Punk, Colm Callanan, Mike Hutson, Animal (Anti Nowhere League)

CHAPTER 9 - AS LUCK HAS IT

Four of us left Bristol in a white Lancia sports car given to another lifelong friend, Mark Austin, by his father Ray.

Me and a guy we used to call the Almanac for his knowledge on just about everything, better known to his friends as Buzzby, were crammed in the back seat, and Austin's girlfriend Marie rode shotgun in the front passenger seat.

Stereo full blast playing Jesus Jones, we set off for the ferry to the Hook of Holland. We were on our way to see an old friend of ours who used to live opposite Austin in Cecil Road, Kingswood. Simon had moved to Amsterdam to be with his Dutch girlfriend. He was an interesting guy and had Spock (Star Trek) like features. He played double bass in a Rockabilly band called Torment, and from time to time we would go and watch him play as I'm a little fond of Rockabilly music myself.

Austin and Marie were to stay at his flat, and Simon had arranged for me and Buzzby to stay at a hostel in Amsterdam.

So at around 11.00pm we hooked up on arrival with Simon in Amsterdam. He took us to the hostel and the guy behind a make shift desk, who looked all sweaty and grubby, showed us our accommodation. There were rows and rows of bunk beds in the dimly lit room, moaning and snoring coming from some of the beds, and the guy points to our beds.

Now we didn't want to seem ungrateful to Simon for sorting us out, but me and Buzzby both looked at each other and thought, *"Fuck this, we're not staying here!"* So we gingerly explained to Simon that we were going to find our own accommodation and we would hook up with them the next day.

`So off we set to find somewhere to sleep. It was now the early hours of the morning and it didn't occur to us that the next day was Queen Beatrix's birthday, and the whole of Holland was going to be in Amsterdam. We went from hotel to hotel trying to find a bed for the night. Eventually we came across a small hotel on the corner of an alleyway and managed to get a shared room. The room was basic, but clean. Being now around 6.00am we were in no mood to be fussy.

After a few hours sleep we hooked up with Austin and Marie, and Austin having visited Amsterdam before, took us on a guided tour. He led us up a small alleyway and on both sides were small shop windows with neon lights and prostitutes in them, looking out and beckoning us to go inside.

Now the only prostitutes I'd seen until then were back in Bristol in St Paul's, and they usually had no teeth, grey skin, and high on heroin, so it came as a bit of a shock to see pretty women with all their parts in the right place. When I got to the top of the street I was almost hyperventilating with excitement. Thousands of people began to pour into the city for the queen's birthday, drinking and waving flags. It was very patriotic and well behaved.

The locals all had makeshift little stalls outside the apartments selling clothes and all sorts of things. It was a real spectacle.

By night fall the area surrounding the queen's palace was ankle high in beer tins, so we decided to go off the beaten track and find somewhere a little less noisy.

We came across a small bar by a canal which was empty, so we thought it was the perfect place. Austin asked the girl behind the bar for the menu; this came in a form of a photo like album with samples of the best marijuana money could buy. We picked a few different sorts and ordered some along with some beer and rolled a few joints.

About an hour later, I was gazing out of the window in a very relaxed mood, when I saw a few motorbikes pull up outside, and then a few more. Buzzby was oblivious to this as he was spurting out facts and figures about something or another. One of the guys outside got off his Harley Davidson motorbike, he was about six foot five, long blond hair, leather jeans, studded belt and leather jacket with Hells Angels written on the back; he looked like a Viking.

A smartly dressed man walked past him, and the biker grabbed him and punched the man to the floor with one blow and then kicked the shit out of him on the floor, much to the amusement of the now twenty or thirty bikers all with Hells Angels written across their leather jackets.

He then walked to the bar door, followed by the rest. Now my immediate thoughts were, *"We have had it! We are not getting out of this bar alive."*

Austin was now aware of what was about to happen as the Hells Angels strut into the bar and all stared at us as they passed by. Buzzby was still oblivious and ranting on about his latest obsession, as he had smoked about four joints, as we tried to get his attention about the situation we were in.

The guy who just kicked the shit out of an innocent passerby was now stood at the bar ordering beer. He glared at us as he picked up his ale. We looked to the floor in a submissive way, like a weaker gorilla would in the jungle. I was thinking, everything depends on this guy as it's pretty clear he is the leader and the other Hells Angels seem to be anticipating what he is going to do. He put his beer back on the bar and slowly walked towards our table.

Now, you would think at this stage we would get up and run, but if we did Buzzby would have been left behind for sure, so we stayed put. The Viking like guy was now stood over us; he seemed like a giant, whilst the other Hells Angels move behind him like a pack of hyenas. He took his size twelve boot and crashed it onto the table to the right of Buzzby; it was at this point the penny dropped and Buzzby was aware that we were in a world of shit.

With that the barmaid leaped from behind the bar and pushed past the crowd of baying bikers and grabbed me by the shoulder. *"You have to leave!"* she insisted, looking me straight in the eyes as if to say, *"This is the last and only chance you will get."* We stood up immediately as she chaperoned us to the door, much to the amusement of the bikers. We didn't look back or speak to each other until we were out of sight. That barmaid saved our skins for sure!

It wasn't until the next day that we found out that it was a Hell Angels convention from all over Europe happening in that bar. I think it only fair to say we had a lucky escape!

You would have thought that it was enough bad luck for one day, but on the contrary there was more to come.

Austin and Marie headed back to Simon's flat and me and Buzzby decided to catch a taxi back to our hotel.

Within one hundred yards of our hotel we noticed a gang of men stood in the road wearing cowboy chaps and leather jackets, blocking our path. I asked the driver to sound the horn. He replied, *"You don't do that to the gay guys if you want to get home in one piece."* So just when we thought our day couldn't get any worse, we realised our hotel was smack bang in the middle of the gay area of Amsterdam.

After five or ten minutes they let us pass and needless to say we didn't surface from the hotel until the next morning.

The next day we hit some bars and a few peep shows. We liked one peep show in particular as when you walked in, there was a guy on a microphone selling the joint like a Cockney fruit stall trader in Hackney.

"SEX, SEX, SEX, all day long!" he would shout, *"Lovely girls, best in Amsterdam, SEX, SEX, SEX!"* We found this guy hilarious. Men shuffled in and out of the booths. I'd never seen anything like it before.

Amsterdam was an adrenaline fueled place and there seemed to be dog shit everywhere. After three long days and nights we headed back to the UK.

Entering the UK we were accosted by the Customs Officers; they knew where we had been as the dogs could smell the hash all over our clothes. They pulled us to one side and started searching the car for any illegal substances we may have smuggled back into the country.

This didn't bother me as we made a pact that we all didn't try and bring anything illegal back with us, no hash or pornographic films etc., no matter how tempting.

After about forty five minutes they sent us on our way and told us to behave ourselves.

It was only ten minutes after leaving the port that Buzzby piped up with, *"Anyone fancy a joint?"* *"Oh, like we got any?"* I replied.

Buzzby started shuffling about in the back of the car. Putting his hands down the back of his trousers, he produces a lump of the finest Moroccan black hash from his anus.

"For God's sake!" Austin shouts, *"I thought we said not to bring anything back? You could have got us right in the shit, and speaking of shit, don't think I'm going to put that in my mouth when I know where it's been !"*

Buzzby just held his hands in the air and shrugged his shoulders with a ridiculous grin on his face.

A funny thing struck me when we arrived back in Bristol and went on to finish the day at The Chase Nightclub in Kingswood. After all the situations we had been in, I felt more threatened in a nightclub on my own doorstep than any of the places we went to in Holland, except for that bar with the Hells Angels of course!

CHAPTER 10 - PHAROAH BETTER THAN EXPECTED

I've always been fascinated by civilization in Egypt, lcd by my questioning of The Bible, and inspired by Percy Bysshe Shelley's poem 'Ozymandias' published in 1818;

"I met a traveler from an antique land
Who said: Two vast and trunkless legs of stone
Stand in the desert.
Near them on the sand.
Half sunk, a shattered visage lies, whose frown
And wrinkled lip and sneer of cold command
Tell that its sculptor well those passions read
Which yet survive, stamped on theses lifeless things,
The hand that mocked them and the heart that fed.
And on the pedestal these words appear:
My name is Ozymandias, King of Kings:
Look upon my works, ye mighty, and despair!
Nothing beside remains, round the decay
Of that colossal wreck, boundless and bare,
The lone and level sands stretch far away.

I've always had a thirst of how and why it all began.
I've spent many hours staring in to the night sky and thinking, *"What's it all about?"*

Being in a mundane job at a factory gives you time to think. I found myself questioning everything, from politics to religion.

I found the Bible a good reference book when studying and I read book after book trying to piece things together. I even read ErichVon Danikens book 'The Chariots of the

Gods', in which he deciphers the biblical readings as extra terrestrials.

Eventually it led me to studying Egyptology. I had many questions to answer for myself, but in fact I found myself searching for something that just isn't there. I did however find that it isn't religion that causes wars; as most people think, it's our old friend 'greed'.

So in 1999 I thought I'd go and see for myself and travel to where it all began, Egypt, the world's biggest open air museum.

Now I must have really wanted to go because it was the first time I had ever been on a plane as the whole idea of flying scared me. Now people will tell you that it's great flying, but on every plane I've been on, you can hear a pin drop at take off!

Just to add to that, on my second trip on a plane was 12th September 2001. In case that date doesn't ring any bells, it's the day after the 9/11 Twin Towers attacks in New York. I remember being in work and hearing a plane had crashed into the Twin Towers. I thought to myself, *"Great, that's the last thing I want to hear as I'm going on the big iron bird tomorrow."*

By the time I got home, all was revealed on the TV. As I walked into the lounge, Sally was sat with her hands over her mouth crying, as the true horror of the event unfolded before our eyes. I think most of us will remember what we were doing on that dreadful day.

I had to make a decision quick, *"Should we stay home or board the plane?"*

I gathered that security would be on Red Alert and so it would probably be safer than ever and so we decided to go. I can't say it wasn't scary. I found myself eyeing everyone in the airport suspiciously. I was looking at the luggage, the way they were dressed and the colour of their skin. I thought to myself, *"If I see something I don't like, we are not getting on that plane."* As it happened, everything was okay; thank god.

What happened on 9/11 in New York was a day that that shook the world and nobody will ever forget. My heart goes out to all that lost their lives and the families that were left behind to pick up the pieces, and the brave hero's that risked their own lives to save others.

My third flight was almost as bad, as this flight coincided with the London tube bombings on 7th July 2005. We were away at the time, but we still had to get back and I remember thinking to myself, *"For fuck sake, not again!"* What a cruel world!

My fourth flight was to Greece and, not being a hardened flyer, when asked to put anything metal into the basket for x-ray, it included my belt, and of course to the amusement of the queue behind me, my trousers fell down! Lucky I had clean boxer shorts on!

On top of that I always got the seat next to an arsehole, and in this particular case, a gang of drunken idiots. I didn't mind them; it was the air hostess that was serving them vodka after vodka that worried me. If she didn't give a fuck, what was the guy driving the airplane like?

So, back to my first flight. Sally, my nephew Lee and me boarded the plane for Egypt and I didn't take my safety belt off until we arrived at Luxor Airport.

Lee was working in travel agents at the time, so we got a good deal, as I remember it. As we got off the plane, legs still like jelly, I thought it wasn't so bad after all, and we made our way to the airport building that looked like a cow shed. Well it wasn't really like an airport in Luxor; it was more like a strip of tarmac in the dessert. There was a notification on the loud speaker saying, *"The bank is now open."* We found that the bank was actually an Arab man with a tatty old brown suitcase full of money sat in the corner!

There were men in orange boiler suits with skin like leather, waiting outside the toilets to give you a piece of toilet paper as you entered, and of course they wanted paying for the service. The airport had orange plastic chairs, like the ones you get in a school hall, and I was like a fish out of water.

After fighting off the natives that tried to carry our suitcases for us at the airport we arrived at our plush hotel where we were searched for weapons and we headed up to our room.

The hotel we stayed at was the Winter Palace and it was incredibly sumptuous, yet had an old fashioned feel about it.

I was awoken the next day by the sound of cars sounding their horns. I was soon to find out that this noise goes on all day long. I'm not sure why? Perhaps it's their way of saying hello to each other.

We got up exceptionally early, full of anticipation and excitement about our first day and eager to discover the biggest open air museum in the world and begin our adventure. Despite the presence of armed guards, which was a bit unnerving to say the least, it's very hard to put into words what beholds you.

Our first port of call was Karnack Temple just outside our hotel, with its impressive rows of lion statues and the odd Roman statues that led the way to the temple. As we wanted to explore independently in our own time and avoided the typical package holiday excursion, we are almost immediately hassled by Arabs.

They didn't seem interested in myself and Lee, but would sneak up behind Sally and pull strands of her hair from her head which made her jump a few times. When they saw her disapproval, they smiled and showed her the strand of hair they had taken. It's all a bit odd, and I think it's their way of coming on to a women, a sort of dating gesture. Most are young men.

Walking along the side of the Nile near to the Temple we befriended an Arab called Yusef. Yusef had his own felucca, which is a sail boat commonly used on the Nile. The last thing we wanted was the whole package holiday thing; we wanted to see Egypt as real as possible.

Yusef was a really nice man; of course he wanted to earn his living, but he did so in a way that you thought of him as a friend. He always dressed smartly in jeans and shirt or a light blue galabeya, and his knowledge of the area and history as you would expect was vast.

In Luxor it can be Heaven or Hell, as the constant hassle from the locals can be annoying; to the extent you cannot wait to get back to the safety of your luxurious hotel.

As soon as we befriended Yusef all the hassling stopped; the locals respect that you have become the property of your guide. So we met Yusef early the next morning to set sail on the Nile. You would venture out early because you didn't want to be in the midday sun in Luxor.

Sailing down the Nile you can't but help but notice the two sides of the river's life. On one side, splendor and wealth, and on the other side, the West Bank, poverty. I asked Yusef about schooling in Luxor. He explained, *"There is a school here, but it's for the rich people. I didn't go to school, but I have had the best schooling ever. I have learned from the School of Life!"* As I dangled my feet over the side of the felucca, Yusef told me, *"You have touched the Nile, you will return and your wife will bear a boy child."* I can only explain being on that felucca on the Nile as a sort of religious experience. One year later, funny enough, my wife gave birth to our son Ryan, coincidence maybe? The mind plays tricks in Egypt.

Visiting Queen Hatshepsut's Temple on the West Bank was enlightening, but I did bear a thought for the sixty two people that died there in 1997 at the hands of Al-Gama'a al-islamiyya, an Egyptian Islamist group whose aim was to devastate the Egyptian economy. However, the attack led to internal divisions amongst militants and a cease fire was declared. Yusef delivered us to the West Bank and we were met by his brother in-law to take us to Hatshepsut's Temple.

On the way we passed Howard Carter's then dwelling, which is now a café. As we travelled along the bumpy dirt road, glistening flint caught our eye, which can only be described as like stars in the night; this is where the sun hits the desert ground. Having taken all this in, one day once back on the East Bank, we decided to go out in the town and find a nightclub, on our own without Yusef.

We found a club called The Dres Tut, and entered the club via some steps leading down from the dusty street. We ordered drinks, and Sally hit the dance floor. To my amazement no Arabs were hitting on her. *"This is better."* I said to Lee, as we went to the bar for more drinks. Now, it's about this time that I noticed that all the male Arabs were wearing high waisted skin tight jeans and tiger print t-shirts, and were firmly focusing their attention on me and Lee? We put two and two together when an Arab suggestively squeezed past me and realised we were in a gay bar. Now, I'm not homophobic in any way, but I was in a strange country and not at all comfortable, so I ushered Sally to the door quietly and explained the situation. As we were leaving, a group started to follow us, shouting, *"Don't go, please stay!"*

We legged it outside, jumped in the nearest taxi and told the young child of about twelve years old driving the taxi, to take us back to our hotel. That was the end of clubbing in Luxor for us!

Of course you can't go to Luxor without visiting the Valley of the Kings on the West Bank. So again we relied on Yusef to show us the way. We met yet another brother in-law, a local archeologist who he called himself Mr Sunshine. He was a rather large man, smartly dressed in a white shirt and beige trousers, and was holding a fly squat. It was only 9.00am in the morning, and already over one hundred degrees.

Mr. Sunshine waved his fly squat at us, *"Come along this way my friends."* he shouted and led us to a tomb that had queues of people waiting to enter. *"Out of the way, out of the way!"* he shouted at the people in the queue, waving his fly squat from side to side, *"I am Mr Sunshine!"* he informed the onlookers. The guard at the entrance let us by and stopped anyone else from entering.

Inside the tomb it was dimly lit as we carefully made our way deeper and deeper into the tomb, until we reached the burial chamber. Mr Sunshine told us all we needed to know, but I was feeling a bit faint as the heat in there was immense so it was hard to take everything in. We slowly made our way out and breathed a sigh of relief when we got back into the open air. It actually felt cooler outside after being in the tomb. Mr Sunshine carried on waving his fly squat at people and we sat down for a drink to cool down and asked questions.

On our way back we stopped off at the Colossus of Memnon, and then back to our hotel.

The highlight from the trip for me was seeing the famous bust of Akhenaton in the Luxor Museum. He was the Pharaoh who changed things around in the seventeenth dynasty. Akhenaton was the first monotheist, believing in just one God, the Sun God Ra.

And of course, his famous wife the beautiful Nefertiti and son Tutankhamen.

We also visited with Yusef, Ramses III Temple on the West Bank; we were practically alone there, with just three other people walking around the site. On the walls are carvings of Ramses defeating the sea people in battle. He was the last great Pharaoh of the twentieth dynasty. I felt honored that Yusef had taken us to see this, as it was off the beaten track which most tourists do not get to see. He led us up some steps inside the Temple that led to an opening were the Pharaoh would address his people; it felt strange standing in the footsteps of the great King himself, standing there looking out over the courtyard and just for a moment I was that King.

There was also one evening on the felucca that I will never forget. We had watched the sun go down and sat in the boat whilst we drank beer after beer. Lee asked Yusef, *"Is it okay to urinate in the Nile?"* Yusef informed Lee that there were some toilets about one hundred meters away on the quay side.

So Lee got up and went along the quay side in search of the toilets. There were armed guards all along the river bank, standing and chatting with their machine guns at their hips. I watched Lee ask one where the toilets were and he directed him to them. We were then joined by more of Yusef's cousins and uncles and of course more brother in-laws.

Time went on and I became concerned that Lee had been gone a long time, so I told Yusef that I was worried he hadn't came back yet. Yusef jumped up and waved his hands around at a boy of around fifteen years old who was on the boat with us and pointed him to the toilets. I didn't take much notice of the lad as he had been on the boat for a while and not said a word. Then after he had left I breathed a sigh of relief when I saw Lee appear, walking along the quay and the young lad following. Lee kept stopping and turning around to the lad, holding his hands in the air and then carrying on walking. As they got nearer to the boat I could hear Lee saying, *"What? What the hell are you following me for?"*

They both boarded the boat again and Lee, being a bit on the drunk side, looked puzzled and asked Yusef why the lad was following him.

Yusef explained he had sent him to look out for him as I was concerned of his whereabouts. Lee explained he locked himself in the toilet and couldn't get out until he got the attention of a guard, which had me doubled up with laughter. Lee told Yusef that he asked the lad who he was and what he wanted, but the lad just looked at him and said nothing; how was Lee to know it was part of a rescue party? Yusef explained that the lad could not speak as he was deaf and dumb.

"Well, of all the brother in laws, uncles or cousins to send, you send one that can't speak!" said Lee. A very unfortunate day indeed.

To sum it all up, as I mentioned earlier, the West Bank in Luxor is very poor; but getting to know the locals and seeing their way of life, sometimes made me feel envious. Although they have nothing they seem to drift along happy with their lot, it's very sobering, and a reminder of not all that glitters is gold.

History has always been a passion of mine ever since a school trip to Cirencester in my junior years, to see a Roman villa that had been unearthed. I was like a child captivated, and so began my love of history.

For me, history isn't just about old monuments and ruins, it's about what it can teach us about mankind itself. When we become parents our aim is to educate our children, not to make mistakes that perhaps we have as children and adults. To progress forward, to get better and make things better for all.

Yet, I find that rulers and politicians ignore the fact that we can only learn from our past to progress to our future. There are so many things we can look at in history that can show us the way into the future, the mistakes that were made that we can learn from. The rise and fall of the Roman Empire, Nazism, Communism, the fall of the British Empire, the list goes on and on.

I think I would prefer a historian to rule rather than a politician; the knowledge of history is there for everyone to see, we must look back to be able to look forward - it's not rocket science.

Change will come, it's inevitable, and it's just a matter of when. Looking back again in the past The Romans held games in the coliseum, for every walk of life, rich and poor alike, it gave the people a sense of well being. And even earlier in time, the Egyptians.

I always think of football stadiums when I think of the coliseum and its gladiators, it seems the same to me in a strange way, the only difference I see is that football at top level is not for the poor man by a long shot, it seems to be a rich man's sport; the average family could not afford the inflated prices on offer for seats, which is a shame because I've always thought of football as the common man's game.

Ok, you can watch it on TV, but it's just not the same as being in the crowd, feeling you are in some way a part of what is about to unfold. I find money in football at present unsavory. I hear stories of children being scouted by professional football teams, offering the parents cars and lavish gifts to get their hands on a young talented child.

I am lucky enough to have a place of great history right on my door step, here in the South West of England. As a child I was taken to the post card picture village of Castle Combe in Wiltshire by my mother and father on a day trip out. For a child there isn't much there to do, but what interested me was that a movie had been made there in 1967; I would have been just three years old. It starred the late great English gentleman Rex Harrison and the movie was called Doctor Dolittle. I was fascinated walking in Rex Harrison's footsteps, and seeing the locations where scenes had been filmed, and so began my ongoing interest in this small hamlet.

Other films have used its unique setting, the Hollywood blockbuster Stardust; The Wolf Man starring Sir Anthony Hopkins; and not forgetting Steven Spielberg's War Horse; and also TV programmes Poirot, and Robin of Sherwood.

The village itself dates back to Roman times when a Roman villa was situated at the top of the valley, and vacated in the 5th century AD. Reginald de Dunstanville built a castle during the civil war 1135-1154, hence the name Castle Combe.

Walter Dunstanville (1270) is entombed in the village church with effigy showing him in full chain armour and his legs crossed, to indicate he was victorious in two crusades.

The castle site is where the now Manor House is situated. In 1440 Henry VI granted a weekly market, which was situated around the market cross.

Many strange goings on, had been reported over the years in and near by the village; ghostly sightings and such.

There have been many reports of a Roman Centurion standing on guard at the Roman built bridge that crosses the river at the mouth of the village.

Also strange voices coming from Parsonage woods? Could this have been ghostly sounds of men in battle? In 877 King Alfred was at his residence in nearby Chippenham, when the Viking King Guthrum attacked. Alfred managed to escape and sent messages to those living nearby to meet with him.

After ambushing the Vikings, he managed to escape to the Somerset marshes and rebuild his army, which would once and for all put pay to the Vikings. Castle Combe would have been the perfect place for such an ambush, so is it the cries of the Vikings that are heard at night?

I did in fact go to the woods out of curiosity, but nothing could be heard, as I expected. Having said that, I made my visit in day light; only the brave would dare go at night fall.

Nobody knows for sure what lies behind these phenomena, but it is said that the few that have experienced it, never venture into the woods again.

CHAPTER 11 - A CLOSE ENCOUNTER

Some things that happen in life that just can't be explained and I've had two experiences that still baffle me to this day.

Whilst I was on holiday in the lovely island of Rhodes, something very odd happened one evening while we were having a bite to eat on a roof top restaurant. It was as you would expect, very hot throughout the day; so the best time to eat was when the sun was going down. We all sat around the table laughing and joking after we had finished our meals. There's not much light pollution in the small village of Pefki, so the night sky is clear to see. Out of nowhere came a ball of fire, right above our heads. It came and went in seconds and we all just looked at each other open mouthed and seconds later we heard a thud.

Our first reaction was that it was a meteorite, and it could have well been, but for some reason it just didn't seem like one to me, but I'm no expert. The staff in the restaurant didn't take any notice at all? When I asked the owner if he had seen what just happened he replied, *"It was probably a meteorite."* and got on with his business.

I was thinking to myself that I've just witnessed something very odd indeed, but nobody seemed interested. Whatever it was, it hit the earth for sure.

The next day I thought I would awake to everyone in the town talking about what had happened the night before, but nothing was said. I bought a newspaper to see if I could find anything out, but again nothing. So I began to ask the locals if they had any information on what it was. Most said a meteorite, but one man said he had seen on the news that it was a Russian satellite brought down by the Americans to land in the sea, which I found a bit elaborate.

When I returned home I began to search the internet for any pieces of news on the happening, but found nothing. I think I was lucky to see what happened that night, but nothing could prepare me for what I witnessed one evening on my way to a band rehearsal back in Kingswood.

I met Lee Williams at the top of Fisher Road, just down from The Anchor Inn in Kingswood. Fisher Road leads straight to the common and our rehearsal room was at the very top of Siston Common. As you walk down the road the street lights end and you're on the common with no light pollution. As we were walking up toward our rehearsal room with our guitars on our shoulders we noticed something in the sky. By this time we had bumped into Bob Watson, our other guitarist, who was also making his way to rehearsal.

All three of us stood staring into the night sky at what I can only describe as two cigar shaped lights, which were a bluey yellow in color. My first thoughts were that it was lasers and that someone was playing a practical joke, but they were above the clouds, miles up.

The objects were still and then they moved around at speed and then came to a standstill again.

We carried on walking toward the rehearsal room and we had now been watching the objects for five minutes or so; suddenly they disappeared. Had I been on my own I probably would not have mentioned it to anyone in fear that they thought I was going mad, but all I can say is that what we saw that night was very peculiar indeed and I have no explanation at all to what it was!

CHAPTER 12 - A DREADED PHONECALL

I was in my later teens when I met a girl called Stacey. I'd been to a youth club, The YMCA, which was next to an onion factory in Kingswood.

It was the night I'd found out that boxing wasn't for me. The YMCA was a place you could play darts, table tennis, judo or boxing. I liked the idea of boxing at the time and my father's friend, Ray Jones, would teach the kids how to box. At first I found it great; I felt I had a knack for the sport, but on that night Ray matched me up with a lad a lot younger than myself and I thought it was going to be easy. Three rounds of boxing with head protection on, and after the first round I felt I was in the loneliest place in the world. I couldn't have been more wrong. The kid was like lightning and hurt me in places I didn't even know existed. I'd had a good beating from a younger chap and I thought, that's enough of that for me!

So, after I swallowed my pride, I found myself walking beside the local park when I see a gang of girls forcefully cutting another girl's hair without her permission, so I intervened and stopped them. They all had Parker coats on and Doctor Martin boots and short hair; it was the new breed of Mods.

Now being a punk rocker I was attracted to anyone who didn't want to play by the rules so the attraction to Stacey was a rebellious one. Our relationship to be honest wasn't made in heaven. It was a volatile one at best, but sometimes volatile relationships are hard to stop; it becomes a way of life and it's very hard to explain why you would stay in a relationship when you know you shouldn't be.

I don't want to paint a bad picture of her as it was six of one and half a dozen of the other; I was just as much to blame as her for our jealous and selfish ways. Don't get me wrong we did have good times, we had our daughter Samantha, but by the time she was three things took a turn for the worse. We were both pretty unhappy and the bills were piling up to add to an already strained relationship.

We would go out separately while the other babysat and of course the inevitable happened when Stacey met another fella. The arguments became more frequent so I moved out to my mother's house, much to her relief. It was hard to leave Samantha, as she was the light of my day, but I couldn't put her through all the arguing and fighting, it just wasn't fair on her.

From that day on I never bothered her again. I would see Samantha every weekend and it didn't bother me that I had to stay in on a weekend as my daughter was much more important to me than drinking with my friends. Stacey never stopped me from seeing Sam as my bond with my daughter was, and still is, very strong. In the meantime I was living at home with my mother and dating my now wife Sally who had a daughter from a previous relationship called Hayley.

It is nearly 22 years ago now that I first met Sally at The Horseshoe Inn on Siston Common. It was a warm Saturday dinner time and Sally was sat at a table with her two sisters, Karen and Nicky. The attraction to her was immediate; she had a dark complexion and a cheeky little smile, and she looked a million dollars. This may sound strange but I knew she was the girl for me from the off, even before I'd even talked to her. And so our relationship began and blossomed.

Because of my last relationship I had built a wall, and it was hard for Sally to get anywhere with me at first. I was always letting her down, saying I would meet her and not turning up; she must have had the patience of an angel.

One night she did lose her patience when I was supposed to meet her out. I was in bed at my mother's when I heard rattling on the window and peered outside and saw a drunken Sally on the lawn throwing small stones at my window and she was just a little upset that I had stood her up. I told her to be quiet and go home as it was late, but she was having none of it (typical woman!), so in fear she might wake my mother up I went downstairs in my underpants and opened the door.

Sally was fuming, and she was now raising her voice. I was pleading with her, *"For God's sake, don't wake my mum up."* She was so annoyed that we end up wrestling as I tried to restrain her and we ended up on the lawn with Sally on her back with her legs open and me on top of her and by this time she had ripped my pants off in the struggle! I looked up to see my mother at the door shouting, *"Mary Mother of Jesus, not on the lawn!"* We all ended up laughing our heads off. Ever since that night they became the best of friends.

Sally stuck by me for some reason in those funny years I had of uncertainty, and it was at a New Year's party at my sister Wendy's house that I finally made my mind up. Sally had given me an ultimatum that if she hadn't heard from me by midnight, the whole thing was off. So, being a coward I got my sisters Janet and Wendy to ring The Kings Arms Inn in Kingswood where Sally was for the night and asked her to come down to the party.

That night we slept at my mother's house; myself, Samantha and Sally all in one bed giggling and telling stories. I've not looked back since, it's a perfect match. I'm a glass half empty kind of man and Sally is a glass half full kind of girl, or as I sometimes like to describe her, 'a fairy with teeth'.

I always kept in touch with Stacey over the years and her and Sally became good friends and at Christmas we would invite her to parties at our house.

Stacey was a funny old stick, always moaning and groaning, always looking were the next pennies would come from to pay the bills, a cantankerous women but had a heart of gold and wouldn't hurt a fly.

She stayed friends with all of my mates over the years and it was the dreaded phone call from my friend Mark Austin that would change things for the worse. One Sunday my daughter Samantha informed me Stacey had gone to hospital with a severe headache, so myself and Samantha went to the hospital to see she if she was okay.

When we got there she was sat up in bed, moaning and groaning as usual, and I bought her a credit like card so she could watch TV. She didn't look too bad at the time, just a little pale and she explained to me that she was scared and she said she had seen her granddad in a dream calling her and thought she was going to die. I laughed it off to keep her spirits up and told her not to be so silly. That raised a smile from her and so Samantha and I left. I told her I would inform my mate and hers Mark Austin and tell him to bring some goodies out for her the next day.

The next day was Monday I was working in Old Market converting some flats when I got a phone call from Austin. He explained to me he was at the hospital and they were trying to get hold of Stacey's mother and Samantha, but were having no luck. I could tell by his voice that something was wrong. He told me he had brought her some magazines and fruit and I imagined him clutching on to them as he rang me. *"Get here now,"* he told me. So my then work partner, Darren Taylor, took me home and I eventually got hold of Samantha and arranged to meet her at the hospital.

Sally dropped me off and I met Samantha outside; she was crying and hysterical and by now Stacey's mother had arrived and looked in shock. Samantha explained to me that Stacey had an operation to remove an aneurism from her brain and the operation was unsuccessful. *"I think she is going to die."* Samantha told me as I held her close; myself in total shock. I went to see the nurse to find out what had happened and she explained that Stacey was on a ventilator, but clinically dead.

Now Stacey had always been a fighter, so something told me not to give up hope just yet.cHer other daughter arrived and being young didn't really know what was going on. Stacey's mother was trying desperately to get hold of her husband who was working in Brazil, so on the advice of Sally, I decided to stay with Stacey, her mum, Samantha and Stacey's youngest Georgie at the hospital. The nurse told us that they would be running a series of tests first thing in the morning to see if there was any sign of life.

As we sat around the bed Stacey looked as she always did; she was warm, no marks on her, it was surreal. I kept hearing Samantha saying, *"That's my mum, that's my mum!"* I fought back the tears, I had to be strong for them, I had to keep things together.

We stayed the night in the hospital, although none of us got any sleep. From time to time and one by one we would go and sit by Stacey's bedside hoping for some sign of life; but it never came.

In the morning the doctors ran the series of tests and she was pronounced clinically dead, only the ventilator was keeping her breathing, but there had to be a decision as to when let her pass over. I had to convince Stacey's mother, Samantha, and Stacey's youngest daughter Georgie that we had to let her go. It took me a long time to pluck up the courage to even suggest such a thing to the heartbroken souls sat before me, but some five hours later we said our last goodbyes.

It remains one of the hardest things I have encountered in my life, to see my daughter go through such a terrible thing.

I was unwell for sometime after, had it not have been for the support of my wife and good friends I could have easily fell into depression.

CHAPTER 13 - FINAL CHAPTER

I was at the grand old age of seventeen when I had my first pint of beer served to me by Ken the barman at The Highwayman public house on Hill Street. A masterful stroke of going into the lounge instead of the bar, so not to look like a noisy sort of lad. I stood at the bar trying to look as normal as possible, as if I'd been in many bars before.

Ken was a funny old sort, he was always bickering about the landlord Barry, yet when Barry made an appearance from upstairs, Ken always smiled at him as if he was his best mate. It was a nice old pub and always playing Bob Dylan music in the back ground.

My first pint of Double Diamond for the price of thirty five pence was the best pint I'd ever had in that smoky lounge; I felt like I was now a man. How I saw it, the public house was an extension to the youth club. The Highwayman, now like many many other public houses is now closed down. It's a shame that all these once busy public houses have been shut down, mostly due to over taxed beer and the soaring rent. Sadly, it has taken with them all the colourful characters that inhabited these dwellings.

If people ever needed a community spirit like it was in the 70's and 80's, it is now!

In 1980 there was a recession, yet you could still afford to go to the nearest public house for a few pints of medicine. It wasn't just about getting drunk to forget your woes, it was the community that went hand in hand with the public house. It's funny how fast things change, and I sometimes wonder if we could ever just stop changing and be happy how we are? I'm happy my children have the opportunities I never had, but I do wonder about the things they will never have? The freedom and imagination as a child that I had.

At the age of ten I was still playing with dolls, in the form of the Action Man. Standing about twelve inches tall it had everything; realistic hair, a scar on his face and little lifelike outfits, my favorite being a diving suit. Yes in today's era at the age of ten playing with dolls you would be called a sissy, but of course computer games had not been invented by then, so it was all about imagination. Children have to grow up fast in our ever changing world, and it can sometimes make you feel as a parent that your child is owned by the state.

There was something good about throwing your Action Man out of the window to see if he could fly, or setting fire to him to give him some extra battle scars, some of them even talked when you pulled a cord from his chest, and it would say things like, *"Action Man patrol pull in!"*

There wasn't much to choose from in the line of toys really, unless of course you had plenty of money. Airfix model making was a favourite, and I had lots of airplanes dangling from my bedroom ceiling at home. I would shine a torch on them at night whilst I was led on my bed and created an imaginary battle in my mind, or made shadows with a torch that would half scare me to death. I once had an Airfix model of Frankenstein's monster that glowed in the dark; half the time I would cover it up before I went to sleep.

On the other hand my sisters' rooms were full of posters of the then pop stars David Essex, the Osmond's and David Cassidy.

To pass the time away on rainy days I would take the washing basket into the garden and make a bird trap by propping the basket up with a stick and attaching string to the stick, so when you pulled the string the basket would fall, and there you had the perfect bird trap! It was always better to do this in the rain as the birds would be after the worms that came to the surface of the soil. To make my little trap spot more appealing to the birds I would squirt some washing up liquid on the soil and the worms would come to the top in plenty. It was a trick my father had taught me and he used it to get worms for fishing. I would sit in the shed alone waiting for hours for my prey and when I caught a bird I would identify it, jot it down in a book, and then release the bird.

It was things like this that made most of my childhood a happy one, and proof that sometimes less is more. I suppose you could say that in one way I had a sheltered life as a child, but it is my childhood I look back on as the best days of my life.

Of course, some things have to change, but the only thing that will never change is our greed, our persistent craving for more, and the idealism of living like a king or queen. It's ironic I know, but true!

When I look back I have to ask myself; would I change anything? Would I have done things differently?

Well of course I would, and so would most people given the chance. The only thing I wouldn't change is the people I've been lucky enough to be around. I've been blessed with a loving wife Sally, and three wonderful children Samantha, Hayley, and Ryan, of which I've tried my best to steer away from perhaps the turbulent trials I have encountered myself.

I've only had one period in my life so far that I could say was a very unhappy time and it seemed to last forever.

That began in the middle of yet another recession in 2010. My business went tits up, I owed everybody money, things at home were far from good. Money isn't everything, but it sure helps when you're trying to bring up a family. It can destroy a relationship however strong it may be, and on top of that my mother was very ill and in hospital and I knew deep down she was in God's waiting room.

I remember standing on top of the scaffolding I was working on in St Paul's Bristol. I was a good thirty feet up and having just ended a phone call to the bank that was badgering me for money, and thinking to myself, *"So here I am in the freezing cold without a penny for a cup of tea, what's the point!"*

I stared over the handrail of the scaffold, looking down onto the frozen ground, and then across the city skyline. Everything looked grey and uninviting, and I asked myself, *"Why me? How has it come to this?"*

I had found myself at rock bottom, at the worlds edge, my empire of dirt I had built was crumbling around me.

Then I remembered the words said to me by my parents on numerous occasions which were, *"You made your bed, you lay in it!"* and I immediately snapped out of my depressed state of mind. If you let the game of life get the better of you it's a very dark place to be. Because after all it is just a game!

I almost fell fowl of life's small trials on that day; it's something I'm almost ashamed to admit, but I'm man enough to say.

I don't know if it made me a better man or not, but it did make me feel like I'd been living my life with my eyes closed for some time and I'm happy to say that now they are wide open.

The message is loud and clear, *"Don't borrow money, it's as bad as gambling and if you have not got the money for something then go without, don't be a victim of the greedy bankers, they are no better than a loan shark, or racketeer and they are not your friends."*

I can see lots of things more clearly now, there is an old saying that goes, *"If you want to keep a nation happy, tell them they are free!"*

In my adulthood I've never really felt free, there's always something or someone to take away the sense of freedom. Perhaps it's just a figment of our imagination, a fallacy, freedom? What is it?

The death of my mother was the biggest wakeup call of all. I could always rely on her to listen to me moaning and groaning about one thing or another, and after I had visited her I always felt better about anything that was bothering me; she was such a rock. After she had a stroke she went into a home, which she hated. I could tell she hated it, but there was no choice, she was so independent all her life, and always thinking of others; so she just got on with it.

I would take my son Ryan to see her from time to time, and being the strong lady she was, she would never show any signs of pain or discomfort in front of him. She was a proud lady indeed.

The morning she died I decided to walk to the home which was near my house. I usually went by car, but for some strange reason that day I walked.

When I arrived and was walking down the long corridor that led to her room, I saw my sister Wendy walking from her room with her head down and hand over her mouth; it was that moment that I knew she had passed away. She would have preferred it that I wasn't there at the time, because that's how she was, always thinking of other people. So in my opinion she picked the strong ones to be there, my sisters Ann, Pamela, Jean and Wendy.

I walked in, kissed her, and said, *"Say hello to Ernie for me."* Those were my last words I said to her. She was eighty five years young.

I chose the music for her funeral; I wanted to choose something that suited her life, so I chose a piece from the composer Ennio Marconi and the song 'Deborah's Song' from the film Once Upon A Time in America. When I listen to it, I see her.

You have to hit the bottom to climb to the top. I'm not quite there yet but I'm on my way. I guess I'm no different to anybody else, I'm just Mr Average.

I have dedicated this book to my parents, Iris and Ernie.

And there's only one way to end it, and that's with the words from a famous rock star, who once said,

"So how good was your life? Good enough to write a book about?"

So what are you waiting for?

CPSIA information can be obtained at www.ICGtesting.com
Printed in the USA
LVOW10s0843300516

490462LV00047B/829/P